Praise for *Adopte*

John Piper has said, "Adoption is greater than the universe," yet it remains an underdeveloped doctrine within the Church. That's why we need more books like Aaron Hartman's *Adopted: God's "Plan A."* The Church needs Aaron's book, because it needs to unlock the riches of the doctrine of adoption.—**Dan Cruver, founder, Together for Adoption; author,** *Reclaiming Adoption*

Dr. Hartman has given us a book that is both inspiring and instructional. He is able to sandwich rich theological material in between slices of life that are compelling and thoughtful. Indeed, the blessed love of adoption ought to be a daily theme for every Christian.—**Andrew J. Peterson, PhD, president, Reformed Theological Seminary, Virtual Campus Charlotte, NC**

To expound on the theology of adoption with any authority, you need the wisdom of one who has carefully studied the subject from God's perspective and then been moved by the Gospel to practice it. Aaron takes us through the whole of scripture on the subject of our adoption into God's family and blends it with his own story of adopting. The reader is not spared the heartbreak that he and his wife Becky have experienced in adopting. Joy triumphs over sorrow. Compassionate. Loving. Well written. This is theology with boots on!—**Mike Minter, teaching pastor, Reston Bible Church, Reston, VA; author,** *A Western Jesus*

This book has implications that could radically alter modern American culture! The theology is airtight and the perspective is poignant, clear, and so very personal. This is one book the church at large needs to begin to live out.—**Greg Dumas, lead pastor, The Crossing Church, Tampa, FL**

The biblical doctrine of adoption is sadly neglected in much of today's Christian reflection. Dr. Hartman understands—theologically and personally—the importance of this doctrine to the church's life and witness. He provides an accessible survey of the Scripture's teaching on adoption and calls the church to think carefully about what it means to live in light of that teaching. His accounts of his own experiences with biological adoption both round out and commend this work, both to fellow travelers and to newcomers to these issues. May this work help you better to grasp what it means to be and to live as a "son of the living God."—**Guy Waters, MDiv, PhD, associate professor of New Testament, Reformed Theological Seminary, Jackson Campus, MS; author, *How Jesus Runs the Church***

In his compelling book, Dr. Hartman carefully traces the biblical, theological, and cultural backgrounds to adoption. Parents considering adoption will find this insightful and helpful, as Dr. Hartman not only traces the biblical background but also opens his life through the process of adopting. In doing so, believers not only see a social reason to adopt children (and do a good thing) but also get a glimpse into the heart of God, who has adopted us into His family by faith in Christ. In the Scriptures, we see the joyful welcome by our God to the orphans, the widows, and the destitute. He welcomes them with open arms. This book is enlightening and instructive.—**David Nelson, executive director and founder, Crossing Cultures International Mission**

Dr. Hartman brilliantly and beautifully captures the head and the heart in his work *Adopted: God's "Plan A."* He balances the theological precedence of adoption found in Scripture with his and his wife's own personal journey of adopting their daughter. This intellectually provoking and personally moving work holds a message needed in the church today. —**Ben Laurence Ragan, founder and president, CULTURELink Inc.**

Aaron places a human side on God's doctrine of adoption. There is no greater love than sacrificial love, and adoptive love is an act of sacrifice toward one in need of a loving father. Aaron is able to make that kind of love very clear as an adopting father.—**Roberto Pena, founder and president, Seeds of Hope Brazil**

Dr. Hartman makes a well-articulated theological argument, bringing clarity to the fact that, as Christians since God has adopted us, it is now our responsibility to go and adopt God's abandoned children. Freely you have received, freely give (Matthew 10:8).—**David Sgro, president and founder, Guatemala Outreach Ministries**

ADOPTED

God's "Plan A"

The Doctrine of Adoption and Its
Relationship to Us, the Church, and All of Creation

Aaron N. Hartman

Deep/River
B O O K S

Sisters, Oregon

ADOPTED: God's "Plan A"
The Doctrine of Adoption and Its Relationship to Us, the Church, and All of Creation

Deep River Books
PO Box 310
Sisters, OR 97759
www.deepriverbooks.com

ISBN-13: 9781937756796
ISBN-10: 1937756793
Library of Congress: 2013932808
Printed in the USA

Cover Design by Jason Enterline
Interior Design by Juanita Dix

Contents

Preface   My First Understandings of Adoption .1

Introduction 3

Chapter 1   Adoption in Scripture and the Ancient World 7
            Adoption in the Old Testament and Ancient Near East 7
            Adoption in the New Testament and
                First-Century Roman World 9
            Significance to the First-Century Church 13

Chapter 2   Our First Daughter 17

Chapter 3   A Theological Approach to the Doctrine of Adoption . . . 21
            The Redemptive History of Adoption 22
            Adoption in New Testament Theology 25
            Eschatological Implications 32
            Privileges of Adoption 34
            New Relationships 35
            Adoption's Place in the Ordo Salutis 36
            Adoption as a Work of the Trinity 40

Chapter 4   Deepening Theology through Our Adoptions 43

Chapter 5   The Historical Development of Adoption Theology . .47
            The Theologian of Adoption: John Calvin 51

Chapter 6   Redeeming Samuel 57

Chapter 7   Adoption and Understanding our Religious Experience . . 63
            A Redemptive Historical Summary of the Doctrine
                of Adoption 63
            The Doctrine of Adoption and the World Around Us 64

Chapter 8   Hindrances to Adoption 71

Chapter 9   A Gospel-Centered, Grace-Driven Life and Family 77
            Personal Disclosure 77
            A Birth Mother's Story; An Adoptive Mother's Struggle 79

Chapter 10 Response to the Scripture's Teachings on Adoption 89

Conclusion 93

Bibliography 97

To my son and daughters,
Struggling to bring you into our family has given me a glimpse of
the Father's heart and his longing to bring us into His Family. You have
taught me to love without limit, to sacrifice with abandon, and to trust
only in God for redemption. I have been forever changed.

To my wife,
You have shown me what it means to struggle and plead recklessly
for the very souls and lives of our children. Through your efforts, our
family has become what it is today.

To God, my Father,
who adopted me first at an infinite cost to Himself.
SOLI DEO GLORIA!

"But when the fullness of the time came, God sent forth His Son, born of a woman, born under the Law, so that He might redeem those who were under the Law, that we might receive the adoption as sons. Because you are sons, God has sent forth the Spirit of His Son into our hearts, crying, 'Abba! Father!' Therefore you are no longer a slave, but a son; and if a son, then an heir through God."

—Galatians 4:4–7

"I will not leave you as orphans, I will come to you."

—John 14:18

"Were I asked to focus the New Testament message in three words, my proposal would be adoption through propitiation, and I do not expect ever to meet a richer or more pregnant summary of the gospel than that."

—J. I. Packer, *Knowing God*

Preface
My First Understandings of Adoption

"Pure and undefiled religion in the sight of our God and Father is this: to visit orphans and widows in their distress, and to keep oneself unstained by the world."—James 1:27

I can still remember when I first started to think about adoption theologically. It was 2008, and my wife and I had adopted our first daughter, Anna, one year before—yet the theological implications of adoption hadn't sunk in. At that time I had only a basic grasp of James 1:27 and what its implications could be for my life. Becky and I had been married for three years by the time we adopted Anna, and I had finished two-thirds of my seminary degree. I was in the process of picking my thesis and had just started to think about the doctrine of adoption.

One evening in the fall of 2008, Becky was reading a blog entry a friend posted about a family's recent adoption of a little girl, and she shared it with me. Sandy and her husband had been trying to get pregnant for some time without success. They had eventually decided to adopt from China and now had a little girl in their home.

In her blog post, Sandy described her struggle with adoption and her new family. She had wanted to have her "own children," and she struggled with infertility. Their decision to adopt internationally came after several failed medical procedures. She described how she knew that God's perfect plan was for them to have their own biological children, and their inability to do so had caused her much anguish and pain. She described her "compromise" in adopting and the pain it caused her to "know" that she and her husband couldn't fulfill God's "perfect" will to build their family through procreation. Adoption, she was sure, wasn't part of God's perfect will. It was plan B.

At that moment I looked over at my daughter playing on the ground beside my wife, and in an instant it all made sense. Hearing Sandy's struggle brought clarity to what I had been reading and thinking about. Adoption was God's first and only plan. It was His plan A! Before anything was made, God the Father predestined our adoption into His family, knowing even then that His redemptive plan to make us His sons would come at a great cost to Himself and His only begotten Son. Yet, because of who He is, He determined to do this regardless of the cost. How could anyone look at their adopted child and think that her being a part of their family was anything but the ideal plan? Adoption is the way God the Father determined to make His family! What kind of misunderstanding would cause a Christian not to see our adoption in Christ for what it is—the fullest expression of the gospel? The implications of this must lead us to reevaluate our understanding of "true religion," as James names it, and how it should be expressed in the life of the church.

At that point, I decided to make the doctrine of adoption the focus of my seminary thesis. It pained me to think Sandy's little girl might grow up thinking she wasn't the special object of love and affection that Sandy and her husband had wanted, with them adopting her at great expense to themselves. I wanted Anna to know that she was chosen by us and of great value and worth. And of how much greater value would she realize she was when she grew older and understood that God the Almighty chose her first! I wanted my daughter to have something to read when she was older that would explain at the deepest and most fundamental level why we adopted her and how it meant that she was chosen, uniquely special, and of immeasurable value to us and ultimately to God. I wanted her to know how adoption fit into the overall plan of God—how her life is a picture of what God has done for all of us. I wanted her to know that being adopted is not second best, not less than ideal—to the contrary, that it is the central plan of God for mankind!

I spent the following year reading about the doctrine of adoption, meditating on it, thinking through it, and trying to figure out how this understanding would affect my life and what impact it could have on the life of the church. I spent the next six months writing my thesis: this book is a product of that effort. May the gospel be proclaimed, grace magnified, and God receive all the glory.

Introduction

Adoption was thrust into the public eye of the American people in 2002 by two famous Hollywood stars. That year, Rosie O'Donnell discussed on her show the struggle to adopt that she and her partner had experienced in light of their sexual orientation, and Angelina Jolie adopted her first child from Cambodia after filming a movie there. Inspired by their example, other stars, including Madonna, later adopted. What is striking here is not that celebrities adopted children but that in today's society, those best known for adopting tend to be celebrities. The question that naturally arises for Christians is, who should best be known for the adoption of children? Who should be best recognized for rescuing children, redeeming them from their lot in this life, and making them members of their own families? The answer is simple: those who themselves have been adopted.

Our adoption in Christ is a major theme in the New Testament, and its undercurrents are found throughout the entirety of Scripture. Our adoption is a powerful aspect of the gospel, yet the doctrine of adoption has remained underdeveloped as a theological standard of the church, and its practical outworking has been left largely unpracticed. If true religion is defined as the care of widows and orphans, why is the church on the whole neglecting their care? As those adopted by God into His family and redeemed from this world, we can reflect what the Father has done for us through caring for orphans and the fatherless in the world where we live. Tangibly living out the gospel in this manner would be an expression of "true religion" that would be undeniable to the world. It is God honoring, gospel proclaiming, and ultimately God glorifying.

John Calvin, in his *Institutes of the Christian Religion*, does not devote a chapter to the theology of adoption, yet it underpins much of his thinking—so much so that he is called "the theologian of adoption."[1] The Westminster Confession addressed adoption in its twelfth chapter, but the effect on the church in practice has been wanting.[2] Other theologians and church creeds have mentioned adoption, but the doctrine has not been significantly developed theologically, and thus its application to the life of the church has also been wanting. The purpose of any theological discourse should be practical application, not a mere exercise of the intellect

---

1. Trumper, "The Theological History of Adoption, II: A Rationale," 182.
2. The Westminster Confession of Faith is a confessional document drawn up by the Westminster Assembly in 1646, and it adhered closely to the Calvinist tradition of the time. It has had a large influence on the Presbyterian Church worldwide.

without ramifications to our personal and church lives. We should not forget that theology is "the application of the Word of God by persons to all areas of life."[3]

In the last decade, well-known pastors such as John Piper, Russell Moore, and Rick Warren have become known for their emphasis on adoption, but its theological development is still lacking. It is my fervent desire to see this doctrine, both practically and theologically, brought alive to the church of our day. My personal and academic grappling with this doctrine and its implications to me and to others are the impetus for this book.

In the following pages, you will learn about the doctrine of adoption as it is developed in Scripture and see how our adoption into the family of God was His plan for His people before the foundation of the world. This plan spans the entirety of the Bible. We will begin with a review of the social practices of adoption in the ancient world and how they relate to the theological development of adoption in the Bible, particularly in New Testament theology. Both the redemptive-historical and systematic perspectives will be discussed.[4] Throughout, I will progressively share my story of adoption and how these theological truths played out practically in our struggle to rescue our two girls and little boy, redeem them, and bring them into our family.[5] A brief survey of the doctrine of adoption as it has developed (or not) in history follows, and next, we will focus on John Calvin—his thoughts and his unique emphasis on adoption. All this will be tied together at the end when we discuss the practical implications of understanding theologically our adoption by the Father.

"You shall love the Lord your God with all your heart and with all your soul and with all your might" (Deuteronomy 6:5). Head, heart, hands. This is the reformed mindset for the understanding and application of the Scriptures. The theology of adoption magnifies our understanding of Scripture in its entirety, and when the church practices sociological adoption and orphan care in the world, it mirrors the work the Father did for us through the gospel before the foundation of the world. Orphan care is a part of the gospel proclamation!

---

3. Frame, *The Doctrine of the Knowledge of God*, 81.
4. *Redemptive-historical theology* refers to the study of the redemptive plan of God starting in Genesis and following it progressively throughout the Scriptures to the end. *Systematic theology* refers to the traditional system of theological studies where a topic, i.e. redemption, is studied through exegesis of multiple noncontinuous passages.
5. I use "redeem" here in the social and historical context of "buying back" or rescuing and do not mean to imply in any terms that somehow our adoption of our children is equated with their salvation.

It is my prayer that no one who reads this book will come away impacted in head only, but in heart and hands as well. A proper understanding of the doctrine of adoption requires some type of grace-driven response by the church in the field of orphan care and orphan ministries. When we image in the world the work our Father did in us through adopting us into His family, we will proclaim the gospel to the world in a new and fresh way that is indeed God honoring, gospel proclaiming, and God glorifying.

Chapter 1

Adoption in Scripture and the Ancient World

As people made in the image of God and filled with the Spirit, we should be about the business of knowing God, His thoughts and ways. We as Christians have the mind of Christ and should exercise it to discern God's counsel found in His Word (1 Corinthians 2:16). Right thinking is a part of right living (Proverbs 23:7). For this reason, we will start our survey of the doctrine of adoption with a brief overview of its occurrences in Scripture and how these relate to the corresponding social practices of the time.

Theologically, adoption is first introduced to us by Paul in the New Testament: notably, in Galatians 4:4–6, Ephesians 1:4–6, Romans 8:15 and 23, and Romans 9:4. In Romans, Paul tells his readers that they have been rescued from the bondage of slavery and adopted into the family of God with all its rights and privileges. The readers learned they could cry out to God as "Abba, Father," just as Jesus had done in the garden of Gethsemane (Mark 14:36). Paul shows that God adopted Israel as His son during the exodus, and in Ephesians he further shows that the adoption of the Gentiles as sons goes back to the predestination of God before the foundation of the world. (This is a topic we will come back to later.) These references are the starting point of our understanding of the depth of God's redemptive plan to make us sons, a plan which spans the entirety of Scripture.

Adoption in the Old Testament and Ancient Near East

In Ancient Near Eastern culture, adoption did occur, though it was not (to our knowledge) codified clearly in any particular legal system.[6] In this era, adoption was solely for the purpose of maintaining one's family line. Its practice existed informally as a formula (borne witness to by the recently discovered Nuzi tablets[7]): the patriarch of a family would claim a child as his own and place him as his heir if no biological heir was living. The patriarchal claim of the potential adoptee came with the promise of

---

6. Lyall, "Roman Law in the Writing of Paul—Adoption," 460–464.
7. Rossell, "New Testament Adoption—Graeco-Roman or Semitic?", 234.

an inheritance and a vow of parental discipline when necessary. The adoptee was provided an inheritance, safety, a family name, and discipline in return for carrying on that family name and providing a proper burial for the parent.

This type of adoption was not only or primarily for children: at times, adults would be adopted after the death of the head of a household. After proving their ability and potential to continue the family line, they could be adopted legally. They would receive a new family name that would further represent their change of family status and social position.[8] This privilege could also be extended to a household servant or slave if no heir was born into the family. An interesting caveat to this arrangement is that if an heir were to be born in the household after the adoption, the adoptee would relinquish his inheritance rights.

This practice is exemplified in a story found in Genesis 15. Eliezer was a slave born into Abraham's house and was to be heir unless Abraham and Sarah had a child. If a son were born, he would replace Eliezer as the rightful heir. Similar examples of individuals being brought into a family, accompanied by an associated name change, include Moses and Ephraim and Manasseh. In the second chapter of Exodus, Moses is brought into Pharaoh's household, given his name by Pharaoh's daughter, then raised up in the house as a potential heir. We encounter an intrafamily adoption in Genesis, when Jacob takes parental authority over Ephraim and Manasseh, makes them his sons, and promises each of them an inheritance equal to that of his natural-born sons. Jacob formalizes it by saying to Joseph, "Your two sons . . . are mine" (Genesis 48:5).[9]

The first explicit example of _divine_ adoption occurs in Exodus 4:22–23. Here, God calls Moses to go to Pharaoh and deliver His people out of Egypt. What is striking in this passage is God's passion in defending His "firstborn" son: "Israel is my son, my firstborn. So I said to you, 'Let my son go that he may serve me'; but you have refused to let him go. Behold, I will kill your son, your firstborn."

God claims the Israelites as His own and immediately starts the process of rescuing and redeeming them from slavery. From the beginning, God shows His intent and how seriously He takes His plan of redeeming and bringing His people out of Egypt and to Himself at Mount Sinai.

---

8. See David Bartlett, "Adoption in the Bible", 377–385, and William Rossell, "New Testament Adoption—Graeco-Roman or Semitic?", 233–235.
9. Bartlett, "Adoption in the Bible," 382.

There is no question that He will make it happen, and even the most powerful king in the world can't stand in His way!

God also directly applies this adoption formula when He adopts David's son Solomon in 2 Samuel 7:12–15. Here, God promises David that He will be a father to David's son and establish his throne forever. God's adopting Solomon guarantees David's family line, and He promises His steadfast love will never leave him. God will give him an inheritance, discipline him if needed, and even grant him a new name: He renames him *Jedidiah*, which means loved of God (2 Samuel 12:25).

In Hosea 11:1–9, the theme of Israel as the son of God is developed further as God shows His unwillingness to abandon His son. God has brought the Israelites out of Egypt, yet they have abandoned God, so He disciplines them for their disobedience. Here, there is an implicit divine refusal to abandon the Israelites even though they have abandoned their Father. A similar theme is expounded in Jeremiah 3:14–22, where the people of Israel are referred to as God's sons, and He as their Father calls them back from their rebellious ways to follow Him anew. Discipline is again part of the process to get His sons to return.

The language found in these prophets reminds God's people of His initial proclamation in Deuteronomy 7:6–8 and 14:1–2 that they are His people. God claims Israel as His own, uses the language of sonship in reference to Israel, and encourages obedience through discipline.

Adoption in the New Testament and First-Century Roman World

In the Hellenistic world, similar to the Ancient Near East, adoption's primary purpose was the maintenance of a family line. One of the marks of the Old Testament adoption formula is the claiming of a child through naming, which occurs over and over in Scripture.[10] Moses is named by his new mother, Solomon is renamed by God, and God calls Jacob "Israel," to list a few. We can trace this theme into the New Testament as well. Joseph, being a righteous man, was about to put Mary away secretly when he discovered she was pregnant with a child that was not his (Matthew 1:20–25). However, he was instructed by an angel of the Lord to take Mary as his wife and to name the child Jesus. Jesus will thus be a part of the Davidic line. Through this earthly adoption by Joseph, Jesus can claim

---

10. Ibid., 381.

to be both Son of David through Joseph and Son of God through the holy conception in Mary's womb.[11] This is expressed in the genealogy in Matthew 1, where Jesus' lineage goes through Joseph to David and Abraham, not through Mary.

Paul capitalizes on this truth when he writes of Jesus being descended through David according to the flesh and the Son of God with power (Romans 1:1–6). Paul is not referring to Jesus' conception when he calls Him David's descendant, since He was conceived of the Holy Spirit. Rather, he is referring to His descent through Joseph (Matthew 1:20). This shows that Jesus' adoption by Joseph had far-reaching theological importance to Paul.[12]

The last place in Scripture where we encounter God's naming people is in Revelation 2:17 and 3:12. Here, He renames those who overcome with a name known only by God and the one who receives it. God's claiming of a people, renaming them, and placing them in His house occurs at the end of the Scriptures as well as at the beginning. We will later see adoption developed in Paul's theology and how he, too, stresses that this was God's plan from the beginning.

By contrast to the adoption formula of the Ancient Near East, adoption in the Greco-Roman world of the first century was codified in Roman law.[13] For this reason, we have a clearer understanding of its operation and how it affected the society of the time. In Roman law, just as in the Ancient Near East, adoption was for the purpose of family succession and the maintenance of the family line. It was not for the adoptee. The adoptee was taken out of his previous social state (e.g., slavery, servanthood) and placed in his new family and with his new paterfamilias.[14] He would start a new life with all of his former debts canceled, having been paid by his new family. The paterfamilias would now be responsible for all the adoptee's property, debt, or acquisitions; have the right of discipline; and control the adoptee's relationships. At the same time, the paterfamilias was liable for the actions of the adoptee and was owed the reciprocal duties of support and maintenance.[15] The adoptee would perpetuate the family name by taking it as his own.

11. Bartlett, "Adoption in the Bible," 386–387.
12. There is debate as to the significance of the two differing lineages of Jesus found in Matthew 1 and Luke 3. The majority view is that Matthew reflects the lineage of Joseph and Luke that of Mary. The significance to our discussion is that the lineage through Joseph is effected through adoption.
13. Bartlett, "Adoption in the Bible," 383–385.
14. The paterfamilias was the family head, who held family authority and legal standing over all in his family.
15. Lyall, "Roman Law in the Writing of Paul—Adoption," 466.

The relationships formed through adoption only applied to males, and the family authority, or *patria potestas*, only passed through males. So, for example, when Julius adopted Caius, Julius was his legal father, but Julius' wife was not his legal mother. The obvious social effect of this was that the majority of adoptees were males.[16]

In ancient records that speak of adoption, the term repeatedly used is *male* instead of *child* or *infant*, for an important reason. In Roman practice, the chosen adoptee would almost exclusively be a young man who had proven his worth and valor as a successor. This individual did not have to be from the same family and usually came from outside of it. Roman culture did not possess the concept that one's genetic material must be maintained and propagated as we do today, so it was entirely acceptable to choose a successor from outside of one's family. Infants had yet to prove themselves and many times would die before reaching adolescence.

So adopting an infant was risky business for a family. The best known historical example of Roman adoption is that of Octavius by Julius Caesar posthumously by decree in his will. Octavius was nineteen years old at the time of his adoption.[17]

Adoption also had a legendary place in Roman society and a pervasive place in its psyche—Rome was founded on it. Its founders, Romulus and Remus, were purportedly abandoned orphans who were taken in and mothered by a she-wolf. A Roman entering the forum in Rome in the third century BC would be reminded of this when he saw the statue there of the she-wolf suckling Rome's founders.[18]

Despite the reality that adoption in the ancient world was primarily motivated by the needs of the adoptive family (i.e. maintaining the family name or lineage), both the Old and New Testaments speak in terms that address the needs of orphans. (*Orphan care* is a contemporary term that spans all aspects of care and provision for the fatherless.) War, famine, disease, and the like made the orphan a common part of society in the Old Testament and the first century AD. God made sure the Israelites did not forget their former state as an enslaved people in Egypt, and they were commanded to pay special heed to widows and orphans. — As are we today

---

16. Bartlett, "Adoption in the Bible," 383–384.
17. Bartlett, "Adoption in the Bible," 383, and Myers, *The Eerdmans Bible Dictionary*, 130.
18. Post, "Adoption Theologically Considered," 151.

This is shown in Exodus 22:22–24:

You shall not afflict any widow or orphan at all. If you afflict him at all and he cries out to me, I will surely hear his cry; and My anger will be kindled, and I will kill you with the sword, and your wives shall become widows and your children fatherless.

This group has God's ear, and He promises to hear their cries. In the passage above, we read that those who turn their backs on this group can expect an especially severe judgment. There is no command to build orphanages; care for the orphan is the responsibility of the covenant community. This command extended even to how the land was harvested. During the annual harvest, the Israelites were commanded not to go back and get the sheaves of grain left behind. They were to pick the grapevines only once and not return a second time. The olive trees were to be beaten only once. All that was left over was specifically for the widow, the orphan, and the alien who did not have formal care or standing in the community (Deuteronomy 24:17–21). Beyond that, a special tax was levied on the people for the support of these individuals in need, with the expectation that obeying this command would bring blessing on the people of God (Deuteronomy 26:12–15).

The reasons for such commands are ultimately theological. They are derived from God's divine attributes, who He is, and what He does. He is Redeemer and Savior. God is the surrogate Father and Defender of the orphan and stranger. In these commands, He reminds the Israelites of their former state as slaves prior to their deliverance from Egypt. God delivered Israel and made the nation His son; He made the enslaved nation of Israel His own. Because of who God is (the Redeemer), He does what He does (rescues the helpless). Thus, God is a Father to the fatherless. The Israelites are to care for the orphan as God cares for Israel. Because of what God did for Israel, they are to do the same for the orphan and widow among them. He promises blessings to those who take care of His children and swift judgment and destruction to those who do not. This is clearly seen in Psalm 10:14, 18; Jeremiah 49:11; Hosea 14:3; and Deuteronomy 27:19.[19]

Adoption is the process of taking someone who is fatherless and making them one's child, thus giving them a father, a family, an inheritance, and community standing. Adoption occurred in Old Testament times as well

---

19. Yeats, "The Biblical Model of Adoption," 66–68.

as in New Testament times. God provided a biblical framework for the Israelites to care for the fatherless that was founded on their previous identity as slaves in Egypt and in God's identity as a Father to the fatherless. This mandate to care for the orphan and widow altered the social fabric of Israelite society, requiring that they band together to help those in need. Keep in mind that this occurred in the context of societies that practiced adoption for the purposes of familial propagation—where those chosen for adoption were those who had earned it through their own successes or promise. God held the Israelites to a different standard. They were to care for orphans not because it benefited them, but because God had delivered them out of slavery and He remained the Father of the fatherless. Again, this altered the entire fabric of Israelite society. *We are held to a different standard*

Significance to the First-Century Church

This was the context in the first century AD, in which Paul expounded the doctrine of adoption. The New Covenant communities of the church in the first century initially were founded in Jewish synagogues within the Greco-Roman world. Paul, from a legalistic Jewish heritage, was speaking to a church in a Greco-Roman world about the new believers' identity as children of the living God. Their new faith made them children of God through adoption. In his epistles, Paul expands the depth of what it means to be a child of God and how this heavenly adoption forever changes our relationships on earth and in heaven. His exposition has lost none of its power for us in our modern world: the gospel becomes more scandalous as we understand more fully and in a more profound way what the reality of our new position in God's family truly means and how it affects our relationships with the world, other believers, and God Himself.

We encounter in the New Testament a new type of divinely ordered family. Unlike the well-defined family of the Greco-Roman world, this is a fluid family based on a confession of faith, baptism, and the Lord's Supper, whose familial bond is in Christ. This family is a theological picture of redemption, alluded to in the Old Testament and mirrored in the familiar social structure of the day. Yet it is so much more. It includes women, not just men, and Gentiles and strangers from other lands. This is not an exclusive birthright only to the firstborn son; rather, all share equally in the inheritance. In this new family, all are on equal grounds as adopted sons (Galatians 3:26–29, 1 Corinthians 6:20).

In Roman society, adoption served as a lifeline for the maintenance of a family line that was in danger of dying out. The family unit included slaves, foster children, and adopted children, as well as a mother, father, and natural-born children. This unit was the fundamental bedrock of Roman society and the primary context for social, religious, political, and economic security. Each family had its own cult worship that had been passed down from past generations, and when a child was adopted, he became part of this cult worship. For this reason, the language of family and brotherhood in the early Christian communities, coupled with this new Christian "cult" worship, was seen by Roman authorities as an attack.[20]

Although Greco-Roman religions were accepting and syncretistic, the one area that was sacrosanct was the family order—and this was now becoming disrupted by Christianity. For the early Christians, adoption into the divine family of God created a new loyalty that replaced all others. In this family, God was the paterfamilias. Becoming a member of the family of God was viewed with distrust by pagans. Jesus prepared his followers for this tension and the hatred and distrust that would come from being a member of this new family (John 15:18–25, 17:14). To follow Him meant leaving your loyalty to family and devoting yourself to Jesus and a new eschatological family of brothers and sisters. All family ties were now subordinated to the new family ties with Christ (Matthew 10:35, 12:47–50; Luke 14:26; Mark 3:31–33). This new family had its entire cult worship reoriented through awakening to God as Abba Father (Galatians 4:6, Romans 8:15). This caused no small disruption in the social order in which these new believers lived.[21]

We see this struggle expressed through undercurrents in Paul's writings. In Galatians, Paul was writing to a new community of believers who had just forsaken their former pagan worship and lifestyle (Galatians 4:8–11). This would have had a far-reaching disruptive effect on their family ties. Paul addresses this as he stresses their new sense of family and belonging and tells of his own experience of leaving his old family for the new family of believers (Galatians 1:13–16; 6:10). Paul emphasizes God as the divine paterfamilias whom we are enabled to call "Abba Father" (Galatians 1:1–4). "Therefore you are no longer a slave but a son, and if a son, then an heir of God through Christ" (Galatians 4:7, NKJV).

---

20. Burke, "Pauline Adoption: A Sociological Approach," 122–125.
21. Ibid., 125.

Under the old economy, only Israel had the right to claim to be the son of God. Under the new one, all who trust in Jesus are incorporated into the family as sons of God (Exodus 4:22, Deuteronomy 14:1–2, Isaiah 1:2–4, Hosea 1:10, Galatians 3:6, 2:20, 4:5). In Galatians 4, Paul shows theologically the adoption of the Gentiles, which started with the household of Israel—the children of the Gentile Abraham. All were under the Law as heirs while still infants—in fact, their condition was no different from that of a slave. Once the appointed time of guardianship was over, Israel first on the day of Pentecost, and now the Gentiles also, were able to enter into full rights as sons. Their new understanding of their new family and their position in it was meant to give the Galatians consolation, hope, peace, and security. Paul devotes the rest of this chapter to encouraging his readers not to go back to their former family of bondage but to remain in the new one of liberty.[22]

We should not underestimate the importance of what Paul is saying to the Galatians. He uses the language of a family with an associated inheritance to address their fears and concerns while at the same time showing the glory to come in their new position. Becoming a believer in the new sect from Nazareth would have meant expulsion from Jewish families or persecution from Roman ones. The new believers were now either apostates from their Jewish faith or enemies of the Roman state. They refused to worship Caesar as lord and no longer held to a strict understanding of Jewish law and customs. The new Christian brotherhood was one of disaffected people who had lost their natural-born homes and countries.[23] They were pilgrims in the world, not only spiritually but also socially. In the first century, this situation created a reliance in the church, a close association and interdependence—koinonia was a necessary reality for them.[24] Fellowship

This flight from our old family identity and entering a new family during our pilgrimage on earth is an integral part of the gospel story. We were a part of a family that walked according to the flesh, but we are now in a new family that walks according to the Spirit. The adoption that began with Israel is now expanded to all families of the earth. We were all adopted in Christ, and He is not ashamed to call us brothers (Hebrews 2:11). This change in status from an earthly to a heavenly family had a disruptive effect in the lives and familial social structures of the believers Paul was writing to, and it still does to this day.

---

22. Burke, "Pauline Adoption: A Sociological Approach," 128–132.
23. Moore, *Adopted for Life*, 51–55.
24 *Koinonia* is a Greek word translated "fellowship" in English and is an important concept in Pauline theology.

As previously stated, in both the Ancient Near East and the Greco-Roman world, adoption was primarily for the adopting family, and any benefit for the adoptee was secondary. What God does is a radical departure from the practices of those cultures. The Father planned the adoption of Israel and finally the nations at an immense expense to Himself and His only begotten Son. Because God is the ultimate ground of all being and existence and is eternally self-sufficient, He had no need of bringing more into relationship with the Holy Trinity. Yet because of who He is, He bound Himself to Abraham in a covenant that could not be broken and which ultimately would be fulfilled only through the sacrifice of His own Son (Genesis 15:6–21, Luke 24:25–27). God's desire to make the fatherless His sons was solely for their benefit. This scandalous, selfless act of God was in opposition to the practices of the world into which He entered. *Abraham's descendants includes all Believers!*

As we come to a more complete understanding of our adoption into the family of God, the result is that the gospel becomes more glorious, grace becomes more gracious, and all is to the glory of God! With anticipation and gratitude, then, let us now consider the doctrine of adoption—but first, I invite you to come with me on my own journey. For me, adoption did not become a central issue because I saw its importance first in the pages of Scripture. Rather, it became a central issue because of a little girl named Anna.

Chapter 2

Our First Daughter

I still remember the first time I saw Anna. My wife is an occupational therapist, and Anna was one of her patients. She had already fallen in love with Anna and wanted to adopt her, but though I had always been pro-adoption, this one was a hard sell. Due to drug exposure in the womb and trauma at the time of her birth, Anna was born with cerebral palsy. When I first walked through the front door of her then–foster parents' house, she was sitting in a Bumbo seat on the floor. Her hands were curled inwards, she was slouched forward, and she was wearing a patch on her left eye. At ten months old, she couldn't crawl or sit up on her own. We were also told she was likely intellectually disabled (formerly termed mentally retarded). After an hour's visit, we went home.

At that stage I only understood the basic truth of James 1:27. If I was serious about my faith, would I be willing to care for an orphan, take a risk, and adopt Anna? But I wasn't ready. I had wanted to adopt for years, and Becky and I had talked about it, but I had a different vision of adoption. At that time I idealized it and imagined perfect little babies without any problems or issues just needing someone to call "Daddy." I hadn't yet realized that adoption would be messy. It would be a struggle with others and within myself. It would be anything and everything *except* easy. I had yet to realize that like Christ's redemption and adoption of me, this would be bloody and messy—but oh, so beautiful and glorious as well.

My wife, however, saw something no one else at the time did. She had met Anna the first week after she was discharged from the hospital. Anna was born at thirty-two weeks' gestation and weighed three and a half pounds; due to her medical issues, she had to stay in the neonatal intensive care unit for seven weeks. In Becky's eyes, Anna was a beautiful little girl, loved by God and in need of a home. After several weeks of conversation, we decided to bring her into our house as a foster child—her current foster home was closing, so we were needed—with the potential to adopt. My wife was convinced Anna had normal intelligence, would crawl, and would one day be our daughter. I didn't share her convictions.

After Anna's birth, her birth mother, Tammy, left her in the hospital and departed the state for over half a year. When we got Anna, there did not appear to be any obstacles to our adopting her. We walked forward down the road to adoption, praying and seeking the Lord's will for Anna and for our family. I struggled within myself over all the uncertainty about Anna's future. Would she have mental retardation? Would she have attachment disorder? Would she love me like every dad wants his little girl to love him? Ultimately, I just fell back to the gospel in the Scriptures: if I was serious about my faith, I had to answer the call to adopt Anna that I felt tugging in my heart. Was I willing to do with my hands what I knew in my mind and felt in my heart? I was truly taking a blind leap of faith that this was what God was calling us to do. So I said yes.

That week, Tammy came back on the scene and wanted Anna back. By this time we were legally her foster parents and had the legal responsibility to care for her, but we knew that at any time the courts could order Anna to return to her birth mother. We loved Anna and were concerned that a recovering addict couldn't provide for all of her needs. The prospect of her going into a home where she wouldn't receive everything she needed was too hard to think about. As much as Tammy loved her daughter, she simply wouldn't be able to give her the necessary care.

During the following four months, Becky had periodic contact with Tammy, and she began to love her as well. She learned about Tammy's story and life, and she genuinely cared for her and her spiritual condition. We prayed hard. Anna needed a lot of therapy and help, and we were the only people in the picture with the resources and desire to give her all she needed.

After four months of contact with Tammy, something changed in her through the love that Becky was showing to her and her daughter. She began to get enough clarity of mind to realize Anna's needs and her own inability to get herself clean and take care of a special-needs child at the same time. Even more importantly, she saw the love we had for her daughter.

One day before a court custody hearing, my wife was talking with Tammy, and she looked at Becky and said, "You want her, don't you?" My wife began to cry and said a simple "Yes." That was the day Tammy let us know that she'd decided to relinquish her rights. She went through that process several months later and eventually gave us the privilege of adopting Anna as our little girl.

We also had to struggle with the medical system. Foster parents don't have the legal right to make medical decisions for the children under their care, and navigating the medical system for a child with special needs is complex and at times overwhelming. Children with cerebral palsy often have lots of feeding difficulties and visual problems, and Anna had both. Her gastroenterologist wanted to put a feeding tube in her, and her ophthalmologist wanted to perform eye surgery. My wife is a pediatric occupational therapist and I am a physician, so the technical expertise between us gave us the insight to see the hazards of those surgeries—both would have been huge mistakes, introducing new challenges and actually worsening her condition. The physicians were well-meaning, but the surgeries would have been harmful.

In medicine, sometimes the best thing that can be done is nothing—but our culture is impatient and wants something done now. At times, this results in bad outcomes from harmful surgeries or unneeded medications. Children in the foster system are especially susceptible to risk, as they may have no one with the ability to advocate for them. We felt so strongly about this that we were forced to make the ultimate bluff—we told Anna's foster parents that if Anna had these surgeries, we wouldn't take her. They advocated for Anna and delayed any potential medical procedures. At this point they had nowhere else to place her. We prayed that our efforts and the firmness of our resolve would protect Anna. It worked—and then some. The county was compelled to speed up the transition to adoption so that these medical concerns would become our responsibility.

On December 20, 2007, just six months after she first came into our home, Anna became our daughter. Our struggle to redeem her from the system and give her a home was over. Now the struggle to raise her and care for her was our primary focus. Little did we know that this was only the beginning of our fight to defend and care for the daughter we loved.

What we had learned thus far, however, was the vital difference adoption could make in one child's life. And learning that prompted me to come to the Scriptures with new eyes. I began to realize how vital the doctrine of adoption was—and how strangely neglected it had been in the history of the church. The stage was set for me to delve into this doctrine as fully as possible.

Chapter 3

A Theological Approach to the
Doctrine of Adoption

The doctrine of adoption is not a uniquely Pauline idea; as we have already seen, it occurs throughout Scripture. However, Paul does expound it in such a way that it becomes an integral part of the historia salutis, or God's history of salvation. The New Testament uses familial terms to describe our new family in Christ: God as Father, Jesus as Elder Brother, and fellow Christians as brothers and sisters. An important key to apprehending this is that Jesus is the only begotten Son of the Father (John 3:16–19); the rest of us are sons through adoption (Romans 8:15). Adoption is how God expands His family.

The conviction that we can speak to the Maker of the Universe in such an intimate term as *Father* is at the heart of the Christian faith (1 John 3:1–2). The fundamental way for a Christian to think of themself is in terms of being a child of God. God is our Father. A Christian's self-image always begins with God and a knowledge of who He is. Then we understand our relationship to Him as our Father, which results in our seeing other believers in a relational way as well. They are sons and daughters of the Most High and our brothers and sisters also. In this way, we discover our deepest roots.

I would venture to say, however, that this is not the common way Christians think of themselves today. We tend to think in more forensic terms of the order of salvation, or *ordo salutis*: a distinct series of connected events that describe our salvation experience, namely regeneration, faith, repentance, redemption, justification, sanctification, perseverance, and glorification. We see ourselves not as having been adopted into a family, but as having passed through our day in court and come out victorious. Yet the New Testament explicitly uses family terms to describe our new status, not legal terms. In Galatians 3:26–4:7, Paul reviews the history of our family, starting with Abraham and concluding with our inclusion. In Ephesians 1:3–6, we learn that God's purpose before time began was to create a family through adoption for the purpose of showing His glory. We learn in the New Testament that Jesus entered the world for the specific purpose of being made like His brothers so that He could be the firstborn in a family of many. "For those whom He foreknew, He also predestined to become conformed to the image of His Son, so that He would be the firstborn among many brethren" (Romans 8:29).

In fact, this family-making is such an important process that it has been the work of the Trinity from before the beginning of time as part of God's elected decrees: the magnificent plan unfolded in Ephesians 1:3–6 includes the fact that "before the foundation of the world . . .in love He predestined us to adoption as sons through Jesus Christ to Himself." The Son came to make us brothers and sisters, the Spirit was sent to make us aware of our adoption and privileges, and the Father predestined us to be children in the family of God (Hebrews 2:17, Romans 8:15–29). So whether we view our Christian experience from the standpoint of God as Author or ourselves as recipients, sonship is central.[25]

What is required here is a reorientation of our perspective. When dealing with adoption, past authors have focused on the ordo salutis (order of salvation) and not the historia salutis (history of salvation). Said another way, past authors have focused on a forensic or legal understanding of adoption while ignoring its redemptive-historical implications.[26] The oversight and underdevelopment that have resulted become more striking when we realize that although churchgoers have been exposed to the ordo salutis for hundreds of years, most show little understanding or interest in it. Yet the concept of God's pursuing us and bringing us into His family so that we can call Him "Abba Father" at great cost to Himself and His only begotten Son brings emotive tears to most of us even though we have only a superficial understanding of what this means.

The Redemptive History of Adoption

In the Scriptures, we see the development of our adoption into God's family through the redemptive history of God's dealings with Israel, then with Christ, and finally with us. God took Jacob and his sons and formed them into a nation of people in Egypt. As a nation, they became His firstborn son. God specifically calls Israel His son before bringing his people out of Egypt and through the Red Sea: "Israel is My son, My firstborn. So I said to you, 'Let My son go that he may serve Me'" (Exodus 4:22–23). He then delivers Israel and brings them through the Red Sea as a sign of

---

25. Ferguson, *Children of the Living God*, 2–5.
26. The forensic/legal development is an integral part of systematic theological development.

His faithfulness (Deuteronomy 1:31, 14:1). God brings them to Mount Sinai and gives His new son, Israel, His divine Law. As we have seen and will look at again, a revealing aspect of God's Law is His emphasis on the care of the orphan. God has rescued His son Israel from slavery and bondage and commands His people to remember where they came from (Deuteronomy 6:12). A large part of this remembrance is providing care for the widow and orphan. Orphan care becomes written into the very social fabric of Israel, and it is based on their prior existence as slaves and their redemption by God.

God took a people in the bonds of slavery, delivered them with a mighty hand, and claimed them as His own son. He then starts to use familial language to describe His new relationship with His new son (Exodus 4:22–23; Isaiah 1:2, 63:16, 64:8; Jeremiah 31:9). What He did for Israel, He now expects to be mirrored in the protection and care of the orphan and widow among them. This begins in the divine ordinances directly handed to Israel from Mount Sinai. Again, as we have seen, God's laws contained direct commands to protect the widow and orphan. God hears their cry (Exodus 22:23). He specifically provides food and clothing for them and gives them justice (Deuteronomy 10:17–19). Later, in the Psalms, we even see God calling Himself their Father (Psalm 68:5). *God commands Israel to be the vehicle through which He provides for their needs and gives them justice* (Deuteronomy 24:17, 19; 26:13). Finally, at the end of Deuteronomy, a special curse is made against anyone who distorts justice for them (Deuteronomy 27:19).

The historical event of the exodus that resulted in the deliverance of Israel and their becoming a nation was the foundational reason they were to defend the helpless. Israel was never to forget their former life; they were always to remember what God had done for them (Leviticus 26:13, Deuteronomy 6:21). Thus, a pattern emerges in the Old Testament. God redeemed His people Israel from bondage and made them His son. For this reason, Israel is to protect the widow and orphan among them. As a people redeemed by God, Israel is commanded never to forget their prior state and to mirror God's work for them in this world through caring for the least of these.

But Israel became unfaithful and wandered from God. He pleaded with His prodigal son, but to no avail—Israel rejected his birthright and turned away from God (Deuteronomy 32:20, Isaiah 1:2–3, Malachi 1:6, 2:10). The story of God's adoption of His son Israel is diverted and becomes the story of Israel's rejection of God's grace, choosing a different path, redirecting their affections from God to others, and eventually being rejected as a nation (Romans 9:4). The Israelites perverted justice for the orphan and stole from the widow (Isaiah 1:17, 10:2). They did not fear the Lord, and this was displayed in their neglect of the orphan (Malachi 3:5). God was true to His word and brought about judgment on Israel for their neglect of giving justice, righting wrongs, and providing materially for the orphan. The words of Exodus 22:22–24 are haunting: "You shall not afflict any widow or orphan. If you afflict him at all, and if he does cry out to Me, I will surely hear his cry; and My anger will be kindled, and I will kill you with the sword, and your wives shall become widows and your children fatherless."

But this is exactly where the mystery of God hidden from the foundation of the world enters in. Israel's rejection of God's Law results in their rejection as a nation, but paradoxically, this is part of God's purpose of bringing salvation to *all* nations (Jeremiah 16:19, Romans 9:30). The eternal purpose of God becomes clearer as we see His plan to bring many sons to glory (Hebrews 2:10). The corporate sonship of Israel is expanded to all nations and changes to an individual call to sonship: "See how great a love the Father has bestowed on us, that we would be called children of God; and such we are. For this reason the world does not know us, because it did not know Him. Beloved, now we are children of God, and it has not appeared as yet what we will be. We know that when He appears, we will be like Him, because we will see Him just as He is" (1 John 3:1–2).

The manner in which this plan is enacted is through divine adoption. For this, God sends His own Son to be rejected and despised in order to bestow on us an adoption and sonship that is purely of grace and not by nature or birth.[27] And despite the emphasis of today's popular Christian culture on the love of God and the universalistic application of God's love to all of mankind, the idea of God's love being so great as to make us His very sons was the last thing in the world to dawn upon us in the day when that love was first revealed. God's wisdom from the beginning has been as foolishness to the wise and a stumbling block to the proud and religious (1 Corinthians 1:18–25).

Paul's teaching on the doctrine of adoption can be further understood in the context of adoption in the Roman culture. His teachings reflect

---

27. Ferguson, *Children of the Living God*, 11–12.

three things that happened through adoption in Roman culture: old family ties were broken, a new family was joined, and new commitments were made within this newly formed and legally bound family. The first steps in this process were the breaking of old family bonds and the cancellation of debts. As we come into God's family, we are released from the burden of sin and guilt that held us in our previous lives (Romans 6:17–18). Our new status is a result of His love, and not of our worthiness. With the resurrection, Jesus becomes the firstborn of many brethren. The resurrection is the legal demonstration and verification that the Son who was crucified, buried, and separated from the Father is now welcomed back into fellowship with Him, and now Jesus shares His fellowship with the Father with us (Romans 1:4–6; 6:5, Philippians 3:10, 1 Corinthians 15:45–47).[28] Our debts were nailed to the cross (Colossians 2:14) at an infinite cost to Jesus. The just died for the unjust in order to bring us to the Father. Jesus is not ashamed to call us brothers (Hebrews 2:11), but makes us holy by grace.

Adoption in New Testament Theology

When talking of adoption theologically, one of the first things that comes to mind is Paul's emphasis on our change in familial status. After the fall, we became "sons of disobedience," "children of wrath," and slaves to the prince of this world (Galatians 4:6, Romans 8:15, Mark 14:36). Yet, the doxology of Ephesians 1:3–14 shows that our calling through predestination into the family of God occurred before the foundation of the world—not just before we were created, but before even the world was created! God's predestination of us as sons is a product of His divine, eternal counsel. This magnifies the blessing of our adoption to an incalculable degree. As individuals, we may be motivated to give to the poor and needy out of a sudden sense of guilt and pity, but a parent makes a resolve to provide for his or her children before they are born. Our heavenly Father's divine love is magnified in that He secured our eternal provision before any created thing was made.[29] Paul helps us understand this in his doxology through expounding on God's efficient, material, and instrumental causes for our adoption.[30]

The first part of this passage explains the *efficient* cause of adoption: the grace of the Father. God voluntarily condescended to mankind in

---

28. Ferguson, *Children of the Living God*, 12.
29. Henry, *Matthew Henry's Commentary on the Whole Bible in One Volume*, 1848–1849.
30. Trumper. "A Fresh Exposition of Adoption. I: An Outline," 66–67.

order to extend His love toward us even though we had voluntarily broken relationship with Him. Next, He named a family for Himself by predestining the adoption of members from the family of the devil to His own. This is the *material* cause, and it explains why Ephesians 1:4–5 is thought of as the *locus classicus* of predestination. The Father through Christ foresaw from eternity past those whom He would redeem through adoption into His family. The faith of the adoptee becomes the *instrumental* cause. Once this faith is exercised, the child is transferred from enslavement in the house of the living dead to the household of faith, the truly living. From that time forward, all the new children wait expectantly for the reunion of the family planned by the Father for the end of the age. This "reminds us that while the gospel begins with grace, its *final* cause is glory: our glory but ultimately the Father's."[31]

Everything is now made new. When we read the pages of the New Testament, we cannot help but notice the change in language that accompanies this change. Israel was God's son, but only in a corporate sense—this sonship was not realized at the level of the individual. God's fatherhood to Israel was a type of what was to come. We can now *individually* call God "Father." "Abba" is now our personal cry: as Jesus could cry to the Father and know He would be heard, so too now we can cry "Abba, Father" and know we are heard (Mark 14:36, Romans 8:15, Galatians 4:6). In Galatians 4, we see that we have the Spirit because we are sons, and in Romans 8 we read that we are sons because we have the Spirit. The Spirit becomes our assurance of acceptance into the family. In the Old Testament, two witnesses were required for evidence to be admitted into court (Deuteronomy 19:15, 2 Corinthians 13:1). This requirement too is met—according to Romans 8:16, the Spirit witnesses with our spirit (not to it) that we are children of God.

A variety of terms are used in the New Testament to describe our relationship with God: regeneration, redemption, justification, salvation, sanctification, and others. However, rather than pure legalities, all of these can be best understood as parts of God's ultimate purpose of adopting us as sons. We are regenerated, redeemed, justified, etc. *in order to* ultimately become sons. Paul uniquely uses the word *huiothesia*, which is translated "adoption," to express this idea. It is used by him five times to help convey the idea that a Christian's sonship is dependent on adoption: Galatians

---

31. Trumper. "A Fresh Exposition of Adoption. I: An Outline," 67.

4:5, Romans 8:15, 23, 9:4; and Ephesians 1:5. Jesus is the only begotten Son of God; all others are through adoption.

Our adoption in Christ and our sonship are inseparable. However, theological literature is full of expositions on sonship without a corresponding understanding of adoption.[32] The Greek word *huiothesia* means "adoption as son" or "placing as a son." In the Hellenistic period of the Greco-Roman world, there were six different words for adoption, and the ideas expressed ranged from adopting truth to adopting a moral transformation to a fraudulent adoption.[33] These other terms were used for non-filial relationships or concepts, but it is huiothesia that is used to express that our adoption is as sons, producing a true family relationship with the Father. [34]

In the Old Testament, we see that Israel's liberation from Egyptian slavery and its birth as a nation make it a son in its relationship to God (Exodus 4:22, 2 Samuel 7:23, Hosea 11:1). God's fatherhood was displayed to the nation as a whole, as we can read in Deuteronomy 32:6, Psalm 82:6, Jeremiah 3:19 and 31:9, Deuteronomy 14:1 and 32:19, and Jeremiah 3:14 and 4:22. In the apocryphal book *Wisdom of Solomon*, the concepts of sonship, salvation, and righteousness are intertwined as well.[35] This sheds light on Paul's understanding of adoption and the influence of his Jewish heritage and legal training.

The Synoptic Gospels further enforce the Jewish influence on understanding our adoption in Christ. Throughout, Jesus is repeatedly portrayed as the Son of God (Matthew 3:17, 16:16; Luke 1:32, 35, 4:41). Those who follow Jesus become partakers with Him and are blessed by becoming sons of God through Him. In the Sermon on the Mount, the peacemakers become the sons of God (Matthew 5:44). Jesus answers the Sadducees' question on marriage in heaven in eschatological terms and relates it to sonship: in the resurrection, those counted worthy to attain to it are called sons of God (Luke 20:36).

Paul also models the history of salvation through adoption. Israel entered into corporate sonship at Sinai, but as a child underage (Galatians 4:1). So while Israel was heir to the promises of God, his condition was more like that of a servant (Romans 4:13, Galatians 3:23). The Law served

---

32. Trumper, "The Metaphorical Import of Adoption: A Plea for Realisation," 132.
33. Ibid., 134.
34. Ibid., 134.
35. *Wisdom of Solomon* 5:1–5

as a tutor (*paidagogos*), guardian (*epitropos*), and administrator (*oikono-mos*) until Israel was ready to receive the fullness of the inheritance (Galatians 4:1–7). During this time, the Israelites learned the basic principles of sonship, preparing them for full adoption. When faith came, God's people were no longer under a tutor, and a change in the family composition occurred. Now all the children of faith become children of Abraham and thus heirs to the promises (Galatians 3:6–29, 4:1–7). This new family includes both believing Jews who have the full rights of sons and believing Gentiles who have turned from their heathen gods (Galatians 3:23–28, 4:5, 8). Through faith in the completed work of Christ, we become members of this family and receive the Holy Spirit of promise into our hearts as a witness or seal unto the end (Romans 8:15–17, 2 Corinthians 1:22).[36]

This understanding changes our prayer lives as well. The Spirit teaches us to pray by coming to our God as "Abba, Father" (Mark 14:36, Romans 8:15, Galatians 4:6). *Abba* is a Syriac word meaning "my father"; *pater* is a Greek word with similar meaning. But why both terms and not just one? The Spirit is teaching us that this new family is for both Jews and Gentiles—both can call on Him.[37]

Establishing the differences in familial language that describe how we are incorporated into the family of God is crucial to a thorough theological understanding of adoption. The apostle John speaks of the fatherhood of God and the Christian's sonship. He emphasizes regeneration and being born again as the modes of inclusion into the family of God. Both John and Paul describe believers as the children of God (*tekna theou*—Romans 8:16, Philippians 2:15, John 1:12, 1 John 3:1, 2). Thus we encounter a filial view of the gospel with God as Father. Throughout the New Testament, many different words are used to describe our filial relationship, but all are used in reference to the same paternal God.

There is some debate in theological literature as to why John has a different focus when speaking of the family of God than Paul does. The major differences in John's language can be explained by a heresy in the church at the end of the first century AD. The Docetists (sometimes called Proto-Gnostics) did not believe that Jesus was the Son of God but a man on whom the Spirit of Christ rested.[38] They saw Jesus as a man on whom the Spirit of Christ fell at His baptism and from whom the Spirit departed

---

36. Trumper, "A Fresh Exposition of Adoption: I. An Outline," 69–72.
37. Henry, *Matthew Henry's Commentary on the Whole Bible*, 1771–1772.
38. Guthrie, *New Testament Introduction*, 289.

when he was on the cross.[39] John's main thrust in his gospel and epistles is to combat this by clearly showing Jesus' physical lineage and physical re-birth, as well as to display Him as the Son of God. John does not say Jesus is like God or earns a place as a son after earning God's favor. Rather, He is the only begotten Son of God. John only uses the term *huios* for Jesus Himself,[40] thus reserving the divine Sonship for Jesus.[41] John's focus was on establishing Jesus as the only begotten divine Son of God and Chris-tians as children of God through the new birth of the Spirit. He empha-sizes the uniqueness of Jesus the Son of God from us as sons of God. John's emphasis is on origin. Jesus is in the bosom of the Father and is the only begotten (*monogenes*—John 1:14–18).[42] We are born again, from death into life, through belief in the Son.

Paul, by contrast, uses both *tekna* and *huios* to express the divine son-ship of man. He talks of adoption into the family of God that gives us a new status, and this status makes us free from slavery. John and Paul help us see both sides of the coin. John talks of birth into the family, with us tak-ing on the family likeness. Paul expounds adoption into the family, with a focus on the status and freedom of the adoptee.[43] The differing metaphors of adoption and new birth help us better understand the soteriological ramifications of being incorporated into the family of God (*soteriology* is theology dealing with salvation). In 1 John 3:1 we read, "Behold what manner of love the father has bestowed on us that we should be called the children of God." Salvation is becoming a child of God.

There is also an eschatological aspect to our understanding of adop-tion. Our adoption by God the Father through Jesus Christ our Lord is already accomplished, yet it is not fully completed. In the first part of Ro-mans 8 and Galatians 4, adoption and sonship are expounded as present realities that point to a future inheritance. Redemption from slavery and adoption as sons become comparative ideas for the reality of our Chris-tian experience. Yet, in Romans 8:23, there is the idea that our adoption and redemption are not yet fully completed, and that their completion is

---

39. Docetists believed Matthew 27:46 actually should have said, "My power, my power, why have you forsaken me?"

40. There are three words in Greek used for describing a son. *Huios* is used for a male son or male descen-dant, *teknon* is a neuter term that could refer to either a male or female descendent, and *paidion* is a neuter term used for a male or female infant or child needing training or education.

41. Vellanickal, "The Divine Sonship of Christians in the Johannine Writing," 69.

42. Some commentators debate the meaning of *monogenes*, but I follow here the historically accepted translation.

43. Trumper, "The Metaphorical Import of Adoption: A Plea for Realisation," 137.

something all creation is waiting for with baited breath. The Spirit of adoption is the inauguration of our new status, but its completion is not yet.

The tension between Romans 8:15–16 and 8:23 is the eschatological tension between the "already" and the "not yet." A similar tension, hope, and expectation are seen in Ephesians 1:3–14. God chose us in Christ before the foundation of the world to be adopted through Jesus Christ. Through Him, we have an inheritance that is marked with the Spirit as a pledge, looking to a future completed redemption as God's own people.[44]

Our newfound family is one of faith and not biology (John 1:12–13). "God is the true paterfamilias."[45] Those of faith are the children of God, made so through a divine act of procreation in which we are born again. In speaking with Nicodemus in John 3:8, Jesus spoke of being born from above, born of the Spirit. John refers to the Spirit as the agent of the second birth, and Paul further explains that the Spirit is the agent of adoption (this is possibly also seen in Mark 1:10–11). Our new life through regeneration is intrinsically bound to inclusion in the family of God. (Adoption, however, guarantees our inheritance and confirms our position as children of God in a way that regeneration alone does not. This will be explored in more detail below.)

In Galatians 4, Paul is appalled that the believers in Galatia, after escaping the bondage of sin, would return to it. The method of rescue is adoption, brought about by God's firstborn Son. We learn that the proof and seal of adoption is the gift of the Spirit. The language and imagery here is similar to that of God's declaration of Jesus as the beloved Son in Mark 1:9–12 and the subsequent proof of this being displayed through the descent of the Holy Spirit on Jesus. The Spirit is evident when we cry out to our Father, Abba, just as Jesus did. This adoption carries with it an inheritance and a new name, as we have discussed elsewhere.

As compared to the sonship of Christ, ours is dependent on regeneration, and this regeneration is received through belief that Jesus is the Son of God (John 3:3–18). As the only begotten, Jesus has a unique oneness and relationship with the Father that we are enabled to partake of through receiving Him and being born into the family (John 1:12–13). Paul deepens our understanding of the process by identifying Christ's sonship with ours through adoption which enables us to participate with His sonship. John emphasizes the uniqueness of Christ, and Paul the uniqueness of the

---

44. Bartlett, "Adoption in the Bible," 393–394.
45. Ibid., 388

relationship. "Paul . . . focuses on redemption from bondage to sonship by adoption (through union with Christ) resulting in freedom for the grown-up sons and daughters of God."[46]

Why does all of this matter? Because our regeneration is not the final purpose of the work of Christ. Neither are our redemption, justification, or sanctification. These are all means to the end, *and that end is our adoption*. All of these steps in the ordo salutis are fulfilled in our adoption, and this relationship with the Father and the Son through the Holy Spirit will continue throughout all eternity. The significance of this cannot be understated!

As we will discuss later, many key eighteenth- and nineteenth-century theologians either equated the doctrine of adoption with justification (i.e., Turretin) or omitted any discussion of it at all (i.e., Charles Hodge, William T. Shedd), resulting in a neglect of the doctrine's discussion and development.[47] Instead, the focus of theological discussion became that of Adam's status prior to the fall, ignoring Paul's emphasis on our adoption after regeneration and justification. In strong contrast, Paul is enthralled with the position of God's people in Christ and emphasizes this by foreshadowing it in his description of Israel as God's privileged and adopted nation. Abraham was given the divine promise of inheriting the world, and this was to be enacted through Christ (Galatians 3:18, Romans 4:13). God formed the seed of Israel into a nation for the purpose of redeeming them from Egypt and thus to inaugurate them into a nation—His special people. This corresponded with Yahweh's corporate adoption of Israel as shown in Romans 9:4. Here, we see six privileges given to Israel under this arrangement: the adoption, the glory, the covenants, the Law, the temple service, and the promises. Adoption is the first privilege and precedes all others.[48]

The implications of the above are far reaching. As sons of God, we have both benefits and obligations. We are highly familiar with the benefits: grace, favor, salvation, hope, glory, etc. Yet all too often, we forget the obligations. We represent the Father and are His envoys and representatives in His early business. We are obliged to follow the Father's commands and obey His ordinances. We are to be good stewards of His possessions while He is away. We are to live in harmony with one another, and finally,

---

46. Trumper, "The Metaphorical Import of Adoption: A Plea for Realisation," 139.
47. Webb, *The Reformed Doctrine of Adoption*, 17.
48. Trumper, "A Fresh Exposition of Adoption: I. An Outline," 68-69.

like Israel, we are to be the defenders and protectors of the weak. When we are through our time of probation, then we will rule and reign together with Him in Christ, but that time is not yet.

Eschatological Implications

In examining this doctrine, we also begin to appreciate the eschatological nature of our adoption in Christ Jesus. The doctrine of adoption looks from eternity past when it was first conceived in the mind of God to its type and shadow in God's redemption of Israel, then sees its beginnings with the sealing of the Holy Spirit and finally looks to its consummation and perfection at the return of Christ. This will be done in plain view of all creation, and creation even now is expectantly waiting for the revelation of the sons of God (Romans 8:14–25). Creation too will be redeemed and renewed when, at the end of times, the sons are revealed. Indeed, "creation itself also will be set free from its slavery to corruption into the freedom of the glory of the children of God . . . even we ourselves groan within ourselves, waiting eagerly for our adoption as sons" (Romans 8:21–23). This unveiling will herald the making of all things new.

We see in this passage the entire universe in travail as if it were giving birth. These birth pains contain the hope of a new life for all of creation. As individuals, we too experience this tension between the already and the not yet. We have received the seal or guarantee of the Spirit of our future resurrection, yet we still live in a fallen world under the pangs of sin. Paul uses the term "firstfruits" (*aparchen*) to describe the seal of the Holy Spirit that serves as a pledge or guarantee of what is to come. This word was also used in ancient Rome to signify a certificate of adoption. The eschatological pledge or down payment of the Holy Spirit serves as a present guarantee, or certificate of adoption, for the future completion of what is to come.[49] Because of the seal of the Holy Spirit, whose proof of authenticity lies in the historical fact of the risen Lord, we have hope and a strong consolation of knowing that in the same manner as He left, Christ will return for us and complete the adoption process, bringing us into perfect communion with Him (Acts 1:11, Colossians 1:5–6, 27; 2 Timothy 2:8–19, Ephesians 1:13–14).

This realized eschatology changes how we address our Father and how we experience the indwelling Holy Spirit. Most of us romanticize the

---

49. Mounce, *Romans*, 27:185.

phrase "Abba Father" and think of it as something a child held by a loving father would say, like "Papa" or "Daddy."[50] But it is so much more than simply saying "Daddy"! In Mark 14, Jesus cries "Abba, Father," but not the way we picture Him in movies and paintings. His cry is one of anguish so great that blood vessels burst on His forehead, and He sweats drops of blood. In Hebrews 5:7, we further understand this anguish as being "with loud crying and tears to the One able to save Him from death." Jesus' cry of "Abba" is the cry of a son about to be crucified. In Romans 8, we read about the groaning of the Spirit in the hearts of believers and see that even creation groans in its expectation of the manifestation of the sons of God. The Spirit in believers groans as well, and by this we know we are a part of this orchestra of expectation. This inward groaning is another evidence of the indwelling Spirit.

But this groaning is more than just groaning. In Romans, we see that this groaning is like that of a woman in childbirth. In ancient times, it was not uncommon for a woman to die in childbirth. The Bible even records times when this happened (Genesis 35:19, for example). The groaning and cry of a woman in childbirth was a cry of uncertainty—was a living child to be born, or were both mother and baby about to die? This is the kind of groan all of creation is experiencing, and in a similar way, it is the groaning of the Spirit in the believer. But our hope is secured by the seal of the Spirit on our hearts. We have the promise that our crucified Savior will return to finalize and perfectly complete our adoption. We are secured by His blood and sealed by the Holy Spirit. He promised not to leave us as orphans but to send His Spirit, and He kept that promise.[51]

As we have already seen, our adoption is finished in the sense that the Spirit has been sent and we have been sealed (2 Corinthians 1:22). But in another sense it is incomplete, and we await the completion that will occur when our bodies are redeemed at the resurrection (Romans 8:23). In Roman civilization, there were two parts to an adoption. The first was a private ceremony in which the son was purchased and his debts were paid. The second part of the adoption was a public spectacle that occurred openly before Roman officials. This is mirrored in Paul's explanation of our adoption in Christ and its dual significance—the already and the not yet. God predestined our adoption, our conformity to Christ, and our

---

50. Some scholars debate the exact meaning of "Abba" (see James Barr), but my understanding is in line with that most commonly held today.
51. Moore, *Adopted for Life*, 51–55.

future inheritance (Ephesians 1:5, Romans 8:29–30, Ephesians 1:11). Yet we have not entered fully into it. Our debts are paid in Christ, and we recognize our new family. But our adoption has not been proclaimed publicly to the world—the world is groaning expectantly for it. The eschatological tension is heightened by this waiting.[52]

Privileges of Adoption

It is important here to clarify what adoption is not—it is not son-*making*, but is son-*placing*. It is not a creative process, but a redemptive one. When we are regenerated, we receive a new life. When we are justified, we receive a new standing. Both of these occur instantaneously. In our adoption we receive a new position, but its full realization is at the return of the Lord. In the meantime, we enjoy several privileges directly resulting from our adoption.

First, we have the witness of the Holy Spirit, which we describe as the doctrine of assurance. The Spirit bears witness with our spirits that we are now God's children (Romans 8:14–16). The witness of the Spirit results in our being led by the Spirit, and His continual assurance of our new position reinforces the witness of our security found in Scripture.

The second privilege is deliverance from fear. As those no longer under the bondage of the Law that existed in the old man, we now have the Spirit of freedom and adoption (Romans 8). The Holy Spirit indwells us and makes our awareness of divine acceptance so real that fear is banished.

The third privilege of adoption is our heirship with Christ. This privilege includes both suffering with Him and being glorified together with Him (Romans 8:17). Many of us think of ourselves as servants, just as the elder brother did in the parable of the prodigal son (Luke 15:29–31). We should reorient our thinking as those who are heirs of God through Christ (Galatians 4:1–7).[53]

The fourth privilege, though it may not seem like one, is the loving discipline of our Father in heaven. Through discipline, we are affirmed that we are true sons. At the same time, we are directed to safety so that we will not be condemned with the world. God's discipline is perfect, corrective, and reforming, and He only provides it to true sons (1 Corinthians 11:32, Hebrews 12:4–11, Revelation 3:19).

---

52. Wiersbe, *The Bible Exposition Commentary, Gal.* 4:1 and Eph. 1:3.
53. Duffield & Van Cleave, *Foundations of Pentecostal Theology,* 234–236.

The fifth privilege, which we have already looked at, is that we can now call God "Abba, Father." In Judaism during the first century AD, men rarely referred to God as "Father" and certainly didn't use the affectionate term "Abba."[54] Yet, we now can speak to God in the same affectionate and close way that Jesus did (Mark 14:36, Romans 8:15, Galatians 4:6). Lastly, we are able to enjoy God and have the liberty to offer Him our imperfect obedience, with true hope for its acceptance. Grace truly does become more grace.[55]

New Relationships

Adoption and sonship are about a change in relationships: a change in relationship to sin, to the church, to Christ, and to the world. This emphasis on new relationships lends further insight into the nature of our adoption and sonship. As those who are sons of God, we are to no longer sin (1 John 3:6, 9; 5:18). Our change in relationship is also described in terms relating to Adam's sin and bondage to the Law (Romans 5–6). As we share in Christ's death, we will also share in His life and will be freed from the bonds of slavery to sin.

Our relationship to the church changes as well. We are to love one another and walk in the light (1 John 4:7, 2:10). Our love for each other is proof that we have passed from the old (death) into the new (life)—1 John 3:14. The church is a family, and our membership in this new family has great implications and privileges. Our belief and faith in Christ result in regeneration and a new relationship with our Elder Brother (1 John 5:1). This regeneration occurs through the working of the Word of God and the Holy Spirit (James 1:18, 1 Peter 1:23) and results in opening our eyes to the truth of the gospel. Through this, we further understand our new relationship to Christ and can pursue Him more deeply and completely. Additionally, our relationship to the world is changed by our overcoming it (1 John 5:4). Christ overcame the Evil One and destroyed his works (1 John 3:8, John 16:33). We share in this with Christ, and through faith in Him we overcome the world. "Overcoming the world is part of the definition of what it means to be a Christian in the first place."[56]

Once we become united with Christ, our genealogy is no longer found in the front pages of a dusty old family Bible, but in the Hebrews 11 hall of

---

54. Anders, *Galatians-Colossians*, 8:56.
55. Girardeau, *Discussions of Theological Questions*, 493–494.
56. Ferguson, *Children of the Living God*, 48.

faith. Through our adoption into Christ, the word *brother* attains its fullest meaning. We are now part of a cosmic family that lives by faith, not a family whose line will become extinct at the judgment of the last day.

Our new status as sons of God changes how we now relate to everything: to the world, the church, and each other. It also affects how we understand the process of our salvation and inclusion into the family of God. The traditional understanding of the ordo salutis, or order of salvation, needs to be reexamined in light of the effects of the doctrine of adoption. This will be considered next.

Adoption's Place in the Ordo Salutis

Conceptually, adoption appears to be the most complete expression of our salvation experience. It contains the elements of redemption, justification, reconciliation, and sanctification as well as eschatology, pneumatology, the Christian life, the work of Christ, and the sacraments.[57] The eschatological tension produced by our inclusion into the family of God by the seal of the Spirit is not resolved until Christ's return. We are already sons who have the seal of the Holy Spirit, but the promise of Jesus' final return and victory has not yet been fulfilled. In order to fully appreciate how intertwined adoption is with the whole of New Testament theology, we will address its importance in relation to these terms and ideas.

The common factor between adoption and redemption is the change of state from bondage to freedom (Romans 6:17–19; 8:15–23). Man appears before God in a state of bondage as a slave in need of redemption. He is bound to the sin nature, his flesh, death, the Law, and false gods (Galatians 4:8, 4:5; Romans 6:16–20, 8:23). Man is in this state due to the break in his original relationship with the Father, a relationship forfeited in the garden of Eden by disobeying the command of God. The Law came as a bridge to start the process of relationship restoration, but it served only as a temporary stopgap (Romans 5:20; Galatians 3:19). Man still needed redemption—he was still bound to sin by the Law, and the price for redemption had to be paid. This price was paid through the pouring out of Jesus' blood on the cross (Romans 3:25; 1 Corinthians 6:20). In order for a slave to become adopted in the ancient world, he first had to be purchased out of slavery, or redeemed.

---

57. Ferguson, *Children of the Living God*, 140.

Similarly we had to be redeemed first, prior to our adoption as sons. Redemption is a step toward adoption.[58]

Justification is one more step in the process of adoption. The price for our freedom had to be paid, and once paid, the former slave to sin now had to be declared righteous. This declaration of righteousness required doing what man could not do—namely, fulfillment of the Law (Galatians 3:10–14). God provides the way through faith. Man obtains righteousness apart from the Law through faith in the one who justifies—Christ (Romans 3:24, 5:9; 2 Corinthians 5:21, Galatians 4:5). Justification and redemption are inseparable and thus interrelated in their connection to adoption. The slave once purchased (redeemed) and made free is now made right (justified) with the purchaser (God).

Reconciliation describes the process of repair and return of the original relationship that was broken in the garden of Eden. The estranged son who left the bosom of the Father now returns home and is accepted back into fellowship with the Father.[59] The hostility between God and man is ended (Romans 5:10, Ephesians 2:11–16). Without reconciliation of this relationship, man would be unwilling and unfit to be adopted by the Father and unable to enjoy *koinonia* (fellowship) within the new family.

Yet, man is still not holy, and a holy God cannot have communion with an unholy individual. We are still unacceptable in His presence without holiness (Leviticus 11:44; 2 Corinthians 6:14–18); we are still in need of sanctification. Redemption, justification, reconciliation, and sanctification are all necessary in order for God to fully save us[60] (Titus 3:1–7, Romans 5:1–11), but these in and of themselves do not signal our completed adoption. Full sonship is not possible unless man is first saved from his perilous condition. Our regeneration is at the beginning of the process, but it is not all inclusive—it is still not the full restoration of the filial relationship with the Father (Romans 5). Fellowship is required for this.[61]

Koinonia is central to our salvation. Our ability to have fellowship with the Father and the Son is restored as well as our ability to have fellowship with each other. Fellowship is part of our transformation from the old man into the new man, which relates to our former position as slaves to sin and our new position as freedmen in Christ. Fellowship within the family

---

58. Theron, "'Adoption' in the Pauline corpus," 10–11
59. See *The Prodigal God* by Timothy Keller for a full development of this idea.
60. I used "fully save" here to refer to the perfectly completed work of our salvation that will only occur at the second coming of Jesus when we are forever united with Him.
61. Theron, "'Adoption' in the Pauline corpus," 12.

is restored through the Holy Spirit, and now we possess a common bond of brotherhood with one another as well as with the Son. Without fellowship with the Son, we cannot be united to the Father (1 John 1:1–3). And without fellowship with the Son, we cannot have fellowship with one another (1 John 1:6, 4:7, 4:20). Our fellowship here is also a foretaste of the eternal fellowship we will have with each other and with the Holy Trinity when our adoption is completed at the return of Christ. The initial part of our adoption is now complete—we have fellowship within the family of God (1 Corinthians 1:8–10, Philippians 2:1, Romans 8:29–20, Galatians 3:22–29). Yet we still feel something wanting.

Adoption has an eschatological part that is yet to be fulfilled (Romans 8:23–25). We have received the adoption as sons, yet it is not perfectly completed, and we groan within ourselves for its completion. The Holy Spirit presently is a seal and a sign of the future completion of our adoption (Ephesians 1:9–15, Ephesians 3, 2 Corinthians 3:17–18, Galatians 5:5, 2 Timothy 4:8). Paul even refers to his own salvation at times in terms of the future (2 Timothy 4:18).

It's important to emphasize that adoption is not regeneration. There are some significant differences that need to be considered. Adoption is not a creative act, while regeneration is. In regeneration, we are created the children of God in Christ, which is effected when we are taken out of Satan's family. This regeneration gives us new life through being born again. In adoption, the newborn children of God are authorized to take their new place as sons. This is an authoritative legal transaction which results in our family transfer and recognizes it and all the associated benefits and obligations.[62]

The natural question that arises is why adoption is necessary if regeneration already includes so much. There are several reasons. Regeneration does not confirm our position as children of God, nor does it give us a guaranteed right to an inheritance. Adoption does. As well, we do not obtain a noncontingent inheritance through regeneration, but through adoption we obtain an inheritance that is incorruptible and reserved in heaven for us (Ephesians 1:3–14). Adam's position in the Garden of Eden gives us an example of these differences. While in his innocence, he was contingently in relationship to God based on obedience, but in this relationship Adam had not been confirmed as a son through adoption.

---

62. Girardeau, *Discussion of Theological Questions*, 475.

Through disobedience, he was able to lose his relationship with the Father. Those who are adopted cannot lose their relationship through disobedience.[63] Praise God!

As the children of God, we are justified through faith in Christ. This is clear in Scripture. It is also clear that we must believe in Christ in order to be adopted. Our union with Christ begins in our regeneration, but its consummation occurs in justification, which achieves its full expression in our completed adoption. Said another way, our justification and adoption confirm the union with God that begins in our regeneration. We are still aware of our rebellious and sinful state after our regeneration, but we have boldness to believe we possess the privileges of sons and thus can approach the living God through our assurance based in adoption and justification.[64]

In the past there has been a lack of distinction between justification and adoption.[65] Are they the same, similar, or completely different concepts? The short answer is that justification is a step in our adoption—a single step in the grand plan of adoption. They both help us understand our position to and relationship with God the Father. In justification, we secure our position as subjects relating to God as judge. In adoption, we become related to God as sons and gain security from Him as our Father. Both presuppose regeneration. Justification introduces us to the society of the righteous, while adoption introduces us into the family of the Righteous One. Adoption takes our relationship to the Father further by guaranteeing us heirship as sons with an inheritance.[66]

All this serves to help us understand more deeply and thoroughly our salvation experience. Our regeneration is not just our re-creation as the of children of God. We were old creatures, rebellious slaves, and apostate children of the devil who are now new creatures made right with our Lord and made sons of the living God. We are now able to worship God, first bowing before His throne and then arising and sitting with Him at His table! No other created beings in the universe share in this experience with us. This deeper understanding helps us to more fully comprehend the scriptural language that describes our salvation experience and to apprehend that it is a work that can only be God ordained, God enacted, and thus fully God glorifying.

---

63. Girardeau, *Discussions of Theological Questions*, 476.
64. Ibid., 477–478.
65. Webb, *The Reformed Doctrine of Adoption*, 17–18.
66. Girardeau, *Discussions of Theological Questions*, 479.

Adoption as a Work of the Trinity

All three persons of the Godhead are involved in our coming into the family of God. According to Paul, the Father elects us into the family, the Son redeems us, and the Holy Spirit seals us (Ephesians 1:3–14). God's adoption and eternal election are so closely related that Calvin at times equated them.[67] God the Father is the one who, out of love, predestines us through election to be His sons, foreknowing what this will cost Him. This is the highest expression of God's love to us.[68] God is love, and His sovereign love is manifested through His will. He wills to adopt us. "See how great a love the Father has bestowed on us, that we should be called the children of God; and such we are" (1 John 3:1). We come to understand from John that God's love is the prime motive behind His redemptive adoption of us. Ephesians 1:5 echoes this: "In love He predestined us to adoption as sons through Jesus Christ to Himself, according to the kind intention of His will." From Paul we learn that our adoption is a part of God's predestinated plan. There is no other cause that makes us His children than His will to make us His own.

Our adoption occurs through Christ (*dia Iesou Christou* in Ephesians 1:5).[69] Through His mediation and His redemptive sacrifice, we are brought into the family of God. Adoption is through propitiation: the debt of sin had to be paid. Christ's substitutionary atonement provides our ransom. Our new status is not a return to our pre-fall state, but to a higher status as sons of God who rule and *reign* with Jesus and are secured in this election (Ephesians 1:5, Galatians 4:4–5, Galatians 3:15–29, Romans 8:17). Our redemptive adoption is wholly Christocentric, for without Christ's fulfilling the Father's will there would be no justification and thus no way for our inclusion into the family. We become united with Christ and begin to share in the very relationship with the Father that the Son has enjoyed from eternity past. In order for us to receive the full spiritual and legal adoption as sons, we must be united to Christ. Once united with Christ, we begin to enjoy our new state as God's sons.[70]

As previously discussed, the Holy Spirit is the principal agent in adoption. He is the one by whom we are filled, the one who enables us to call out to the Father as Abba. He is also known to us as the Spirit of adop-

---

67. Braeutigam, "Adopted by the Triune God,"166.
68. D. M. Lloyd-Jones, *God's Ultimate Purpose*, 112.
69. Braeutigam, "Adopted by the Triune God," 167.
70. Ibid., 167–168.

tion (Romans 8:15). The Holy Spirit communicates to and assures us of our new status in the family of God.

Today, we do not appreciate the intimacy of the word *Abba* and thus its significance. The first words of a child were usually Mommy (*Ima*) or Daddy (*Abba*), and these were babbled by infants to their mother or father. As newborns, we now can babble to our Father who will hear us and feed us (1 Peter 2:2). The Holy Spirit witnesses to the reality of our adoption, enabling us to intellectually, as well as emotionally, realize what has happened. Truly, we can now cry out to our Father who hears us.[71]

Most of us will not appreciate the significance of the last few paragraphs, so let me state it as plainly as I can: we *now share in the Trinity*. This fact is beyond any comprehension and can only result in our giving God glory and praise! This unfathomable reality was *meant* to inspire such praise (Ephesians 1:4–14). We have become partakers of the divine nature (2 Peter 1:3–4). We are admitted into the fellowship of the glorious Trinity. In this way, we begin our fellowship with the Father, by the Son, through the Holy Spirit, fellowship that will continue throughout all eternity. This divine work is purely God initiated, God centered, and God glorifying![72]

---

71. Braeutigam, "Adopted by the Triune God," 165–173.
72. Ibid., 173–174.

Chapter 4

Deepening Theology Through Our Adoptions

We have seen from the Scriptures that God's primary purpose from eternity past has been to bring us into His family. And this has a profoundly practical impact. If our churches saw our brotherhood in the family of faith as primarily existing *through adoption*, would not the care of orphans, including adoption, become a priority in the life of our churches? If we, like Jesus, see and know what our Father is doing, we will desire to image on earth what He is doing and has done in us by the Spirit. And what our Father has been doing is fighting for the estranged fatherless, making them sons and daughters. But this causes conflict, conflict within ourselves and with our old families. Because of this, conflict becomes a characteristic of the Christian life. The Deceiver wants to win us back because he knows he has lost and his time is short (Revelation 12:12).

Our first adoption story is not just a story of how we changed Anna's life. It is also about how we were changed forever by adopting her. When I first submitted myself to James 1:27 in a very superficial way and started the process of rescuing and redeeming a child, I had no idea where it would take me and my family. Living out the gospel while studying it has transformed our lives and our comprehension of what the gospel truly means. When we first started to love Anna and give her a new life, we had no idea that we would come to an ever-deepening understanding of God's love for us and our new life in Him.

I can now look back at my life before Anna and honestly say I never really knew how to love prior to adopting her. Everyone I've ever loved always gave me something in return. My parents gave me a home, food, and while in college, a small allowance. My wife gives me self-satisfaction—I'm such a great guy that she wanted to marry me. She boosts my ego by telling me how great a husband and father I am for providing for my family at home, and she continues to give me something in return for my love for her.

But Anna is different. My love for her has cost me. Emotionally, it cost me in the beginning while we were trying to adopt her. It continues to do so. I struggle today with what her future will look like, how her future husband will treat and care for her, and how the world around her will respond to her special needs. Financially, it costs me. Her therapy and equipment are expensive, and we monthly put away money for future expenses. Since the day I met Anna, my wife and I have been pouring our lives into her, and we have been changed forever. Before Anna, I never knew what it meant to love unconditionally without any expectation of anything in return. My heart has become softened to the plight of children in general and that of orphans in particular. But more importantly, I've come to a deeper understanding of what it cost God to rescue us and make us His children.

I've experienced in an infinitely small measure what it cost God to redeem me, and I have seen more clearly how His eternal plan before time began was always bent on redeeming a people to Himself. I've become weaker and vulnerable yet more fully alive. I've been forced to look outside of myself and focus on another with such love and compassion that there isn't anything I wouldn't do for her, and all the while without any expectation of repayment. But the ways of God are higher than our ways, and His thoughts higher than our thoughts. Through pouring myself out for Anna, I've come to know my heavenly Father in a deeper way. The gospel now means much more to me than before. It has become palpable and real, not just a catchphrase to motivate us to service. Because of who God is, He redeems. Because of what He's done for me, I am to mirror His works in the earth. Heart, mind, hands.

As we engage our minds with the gospel, a change of heart occurs. As our hearts are softened by the gospel, a grace-driven response results in obedience to God's commands and doing the work of our Father on earth. As we do this, our understanding becomes enlightened and further deepened, which softens our hearts further, resulting in a deepening comprehension of grace. In response, we desire even more to obey. Or as St. Augustine once said, "I seek not to understand in order to obey but I obey in order to understand."

I have also come face-to-face with Jesus and been changed by the encounter, with a resulting deeper knowledge of Him. How? In Matthew 25, Jesus teaches about the final judgment. He parallels our treatment of the hungry, poor, abandoned, and imprisoned with our treatment of Himself in such an intimate manner that He equates caring for "the least of these" with caring for Him. In a real, tangible, and inexplicable way that is above knowledge, our care for the least of these provides us with a face-to-face encounter with our risen Lord. All who met Jesus in the Scriptures were changed by the encounter, and we are changed by it today. Our struggle to redeem Anna, then our second daughter, and finally a little boy whose unusual story I will later relate, and to make them our own, has changed us through our encountering Christ in the midst of the struggle. We've had to trust God and seek His intervention time and time again.

Abigail, our second daughter, represents one of the many miracles in this journey. Her story was similar to her sister's in many ways: a drug-exposed baby abandoned at the hospital. One day in 2008, Becky and I were talking about expanding our family, but we were not sure what that would look like. A good friend of Becky's was a physical therapist in Florida, and one of her patients, who was in foster care, was going up for adoption. She texted Becky a picture of a cute little two-year-old girl with the caption "Adopt me." We took her advice. As usual, there was a struggle: we were now living in Virginia, and Florida doesn't adopt out of state, so our chances were close to nil. Several months earlier, when Becky was researching the situation, she was referred to a gentleman who was a local adoption advocate. She talked about our story, and he gave her suggestions on how to proceed. Several months later, there was a meeting of the county child placement board to hear our petition for Abigail. The board heard Abigail's foster mom's petition and then let her leave—it was an unusual out-of-state petition they didn't plan on granting. However, that day the gentleman my wife had talked to months earlier just happened to be one of the individuals on the panel. He followed the foster mom out after her opportunity to speak and asked her if the family from out of state was the same one he'd spoken with over the phone. She confirmed this and was able to share a little more about why she felt like our family was a good placement for Abigail. When he went back into the meeting he encouraged the panel to reconsider our family in spite of the fact that we were from out of state and actually swayed the panel to choose our family for placement even though it was against all their protocols.

Stories like this have become the norm for us. Building our family has been hard and challenging, but at the same time, we've experientially grown closer to God, and we've learned through struggling to rescue our children to what great lengths parents are willing to go in order to rescue their children. This pales in comparison to what God has done for us, but it has deepened our understanding of what the gospel is and what it means. At a basic level, the good news is that God saves those in needs of a Savior. On a deeper level, it is that God goes to great lengths, at great expense to Himself and harm to His Son, to redeem us. This He planned before time began and the world was made.

Early on, I realized that I did not truly understand the doctrine of adoption in the Scriptures. As I made it the focus of much study, I realized that there is a reason for this: historically, the doctrine has been underdeveloped to the point of neglect. In the following chapters, we will explore the historical development of the theology of adoption.

Chapter 5

The Historical Development of
Adoption Theology

It is hard to believe that in two thousand years of theological reflection, the church has produced only six confessions that include a chapter on the doctrine of adoption. Very little has been written exclusively on adoption, and the silence is deafening. This lack of development is even more stunning given the fact that care of the fatherless is one of the three pillars of religion mentioned in James 1:27. As Christians, our lives are impoverished by a lack of understanding of this important doctrine, both as it relates to our own standing with God and as it relates to the practical outworking of our lives. This chapter will summarize the historical development of adoption theology and show the need to rediscover this often forgotten jewel of the church.

We first see the doctrine of adoption in the body of ecclesiastical writings in the theology of Irenaeus in the second century AD. He discusses our adoption as sons in the context of the fatherhood of God, but does not expound on the subject of sonship and the placing of us as sons. The result was an emphasis only of the fatherhood of God without a development of what sonship entails. Origen, in the third century, showed an interest in the family themes of Scripture, but it was not until Athanasius in the fourth century that a systematic study of these took place. In the eastern church at that time, however, the predominant focus was on John's model of rebirth and not on the Pauline model of adoption. Subsequently, the Johannine model became the standard for studies of the family relationships in Christ.[73]

In the western church, St. Augustine focused on the sovereignty of God. The theology of God as Father, for the most part, was passed over. Modern scholars have noted that Augustine's ideas of deification and mystical union in Christ are similar to the ideas of Athanasius, but in the millennium that followed, theology in the West centered on God's sovereignty. This is epitomized in Anselm's *Cur Deus Homo*, where a judicial view

---

73. Trumper, "The Theological History of Adoption I: An Account," 15–16.

of redemption is espoused. The theology of God's sovereignty thus had a legalistic development, which Anselm expressed in his understanding of the infinite satisfaction of Christ. This judicial and legalistic understanding continued to be developed until the time of the Reformation. Luther, an Augustinian monk, was so influenced by this view of God that he only thought of God in terms of a judge. It wasn't until Luther understood justification by faith alone through grace alone that he was able to get out from under the weight of the Law, and later in his life it was only after he became a father himself that he started to appreciate the love and comfort that comes from knowing God as Father.

In contrast to Luther, Calvin emphasized the fatherhood of God to such a degree that he became "*the* theologian of adoption," according to Trumper.[74] However, in Calvin's seminal work, Institutes of the *Christian Religion*, he does not devote a section to the doctrine of adoption, instead alluding to it throughout his work. As the primary Reformation theologian, his thoughts influenced those who would follow. In *Institutes*, he asserts that the entire gospel is embraced in adoption. But since the book does not have a chapter devoted to adoption, later scholars have believed that adoption was not that crucial to Calvin, and its importance and further development were left undone.[75] We will return to discuss Calvin's thoughts a little more thoroughly after finishing this brief historical summary.

Both Peter Martyr Vermigli, who corresponded with Calvin, and John Knox, who lived in Geneva several years while Calvin was there, speak of adoption in their writings. Knox mentioned it in relationship to predestination, and Martyr's theology resonated with a familial tone, but it was not long until Reformed theology lost any pervading sense of the doctrine of adoption.[76] Part of this had to do with the influence of Francis Turretin. Turretin equated adoption with justification, replacing the biblical picture of a family relationship in understanding salvation and going back to the more forensic and legal one that prevailed in the church prior to the Reformation. His three-volume *Theologia Elentica* became the standard textbook for Reformed universities and seminaries for two hundred years, influencing the pastors and theologians trained there.[77]

During the same time period, the Westminster Divines produced their confession of faith, which *did* include a chapter on the doctrine of

---

74. Trumper, "The Theological History of Adoption I: An Account," 182.
75. Ibid., 13–18.
76. Ibid., 20–21.
77. Kelly, "Adoption: An Underdeveloped Heritage of the Westminster Standards," 112.

adoption. The twelfth chapter of the Westminster Confession of Faith states:

> God guarantees the gracious gift of adoption for all those who are justified in and for the sake of His only son, Jesus Christ. Those adopted enjoy the liberties and privileges of God's children, have His name put on them, receive the Spirit of adoption, have access to the throne of grace with boldness, and are enabled to cry, Abba, Father. They are pitied, protected, provided for, and disciplined by Him as a Father. They are never cast off, however, and are sealed until the day of redemption and inherit the promises as heirs of everlasting salvation.[78]

This chapter places a clear emphasis on the doctrine of adoption and its importance to the believer. Chapters 3 and 18 of the confession also mention adoption in relation to God's eternal decrees (chapter 3) and assurance (chapter 18). However, this understanding and emphasis were not carried on by future theologians.

The nineteenth-century Princeton theologian Charles Hodge continued the trend of underdeveloping adoption in his *Systematic Theology*. He saw adoption as a part of redemption and put his emphasis on redemption in his writings.[79] Out of 339 references to adoption in his *Systematic Theology*, fewer than twenty referred to adoption in the filial sense. The Baptist Reformed theologian A.H. Strong, of the same era, placed adoption under regeneration and justification[80] Robert Candlish, another nineteenth-century theologian, and Robert Webb in the twentieth century, both credit the influence of Turretin and his seminary texts with deemphasizing the doctrine of adoption by equating it with justification.[81]

So why this glaring neglect? How could such a key doctrine become so lost in our historical understanding? There is not space here to fully develop this, but historically, it appears that the theological battle of the times determines which doctrines get the most thought, energy, and contemplation by the church. In the first four centuries of the church, the identity and essence of Jesus were the first battle line. Was He merely a man, was He a man on whom the Spirit of God rested, or was He indeed the God-Man? In the seventh and eighth centuries, an Adoptionist con-

---

78. Kelly, McClure, and Rollinson, *The Westminster Confession of Faith*, 35.
79. Hodge, *Systematic Theology*, vol. 2, 517–518.
80. Strong, *Systematic Theology*, 812, 856.
81. Candlish, *The Fatherhood of God*, 238, and Kelly, "Adoption: An Underdeveloped Heritage of the Westminster Standards," 112.

troversy raged—but this one dealt with Jesus' adoption, not ours. At the heart of this controversy was the theory that the *Logos* was the only begotten Son of God, but the man Jesus was the son of God by adoption. This heresy may have caused a degree of hesitancy in future theologians to develop a doctrine that might be seen as associated with it. The Reformers, during their time, were struggling to recover the basis of our justification (while at the same time struggling for their very lives). The time following this found most theologians debating soteriology, justification, and the Lord's Supper. Unfortunately, the emphasis on the doctrine of justification resulted in a neglect of that of adoption.

The next significant distraction from expounding the doctrine of adoption came in the 1860s in the form of a familial focus on the fatherhood of God. The classic expression of this occurred in a debate in which Dr. Candlish refuted Dr. Crawford's stance on the universal fatherhood of God.[82] In this thinking, God is the Father of all and in the end will bring all into His family.[83] Robert Webb showed how this so-called "New Theology," through its inappropriate understanding of the fatherhood of God, degenerated into the corollaries of the universal childhood of sinners, the universal brotherhood of man, and the solidarity of the human race.[84] This thinking deconstructed the entire doctrine of atonement by erasing the necessity for Christ's propitiatory sacrifice, the concept of eternal punishment, and the need to punish sin.[85] (The recent book *Love Wins* has reignited interest in this idea of the universal fatherhood of God.)

For centuries, controversies and social unrest have hindered a comprehensive development of the doctrine of adoption.[86] This has been to our detriment personally and theologically. (For one thing, a more thorough development of the doctrine of adoption in the past could have thwarted the development of erroneous doctrine in the church—but space here does not permit exploring this.[87])

The lack of extensive exegesis of the doctrine of adoption from the pastorate and the seminary persisted until the nineteenth century with the writings of Robert Candlish, followed by those of John Girardeau and Robert A. Webb in the twentieth century. Webb, Candlish, and Girardeau

---

82. Candlish, *The Fatherhood of God.*
83. Trumper, "The Theological History of Adoption II: A Rationale," 179–181.
84. Webb, *The Reformed Doctrine of Adoption,* 23.
85. Ibid., 22–25.
86. Trumper, "The Theological History of Adoption II: A Rationale," 201.
87. Webb, *The Reformed Doctrine of Adoption,* 27.

have been the only major modern theologians to discuss the doctrine of adoption, but it still remains largely undiscovered by modern pastors and seminaries. Suffice it to say there is a historical precedent for this trend of neglect!

The one exception to this trend, as we have already seen, is Calvin. Adoption was central to his understanding, and in that, he is still leading the way for us today.

The Theologian of Adoption: John Calvin

In John Calvin's day, justification by faith had just had its renaissance, and it was being directly challenged by the Catholic Church. This onslaught had its full expression in the Council of Trent (1545–1563). Calvin, therefore, spent his energies developing and defending this newly rediscovered jewel. Often overlooked, however, is the importance of the doctrine of adoption in Calvin's thinking. It is a misconception that only what Calvin valued most was given chapter headings in *Institutes*. "With the renaissance in Calvin studies . . . we are learning that the ascertaining of the importance of a doctrine for Calvin is determined not by the number of chapters allotted to its discussion but how pervasively it is referred to throughout his work."[88]

From this vantage point, when reading the *Institutes*, we see that adoption was far more crucial to him than previously thought.[89]

John Calvin, according to J. Scott-Lidgett, made more of the fatherhood of God than any other Reformation writer and was the first theologian since Iraneus to do so.[90] His exegesis of our familial relationship to God focused primarily on the fatherhood of God. Calvin saw adoption as a process in which all three persons of the Trinity were involved. The Father is the agent in adoption; the Son performs the work of atonement, securing the grounds for adoption, and the Holy Spirit is the Spirit of adoption who functions to create in us "filial confidence," or assurance of our newly adopted state.[91] The privilege of adoption is constituted by grace as a consequence of the "free benevolence of God" (*Institutes* 3:1:3).

Calvin saw all humankind as the posterity of God due to our creation in the *Imago Dei*, but he argued that this was lost in the fall. We were

---

88. Trumper, "The Theological History of Adoption. II: A Rationale," 183.
89. Ibid., 182–184.
90. Lidgett, *The Fatherhood of God in Christian Truth and Life*, 253.
91. Westhead, "Adoption in the Thought of John Calvin," 102–106

disowned as sons due to Adam's sins. The message of the cross is that God is redeeming us back to Himself through Christ.[92] Thus Calvin saw adoption as redemptive sonship. No adoption occurs outside of Christ and His work on the cross (*Institutes* 2:6:1). Only through Christ can we with confidence address God as Father. As such, adoption is the category used to describe one who is released from the Law. It is the fruit of the cross that we must humbly embrace if our sonship is to be restored (*Institutes* 2:6:1). Furthermore, the incarnation makes possible the atonement, which then restores us to God as our Father and us as His sons. "The incarnation is itself an event upon which our adoption is founded."[93] Christ took our nature upon Himself in order to impart to us what was His—heirship of the heavenly kingdom (*Institutes* 2:2:2). His becoming the Son of Man makes us the sons of God with Him. His taking on our mortality enables us to partake of his immortality. He took our poverty and suffering, resulting in the transference of His wealth to us. "By taking the weight of our iniquity upon himself (which oppressed us) he has clothed us with his righteousness" (Institutes 4:17:2). Thus, redemptive sonship is clearly portrayed.

Here, the Holy Spirit helps with our weakness. These lofty ideas seem hard to grasp and believe, yet they are true. The Holy Spirit is called the Spirit of adoption for this very reason. He is the witness and guarantee to us of the free and generous gift of our adoption by God (*Institutes* 3:1:3). Calvin believed that the assurance of salvation was the essence of saving faith. This "assurance of our sonship comes from leaning and resting upon the knowledge of the divine favor towards us as revealed in the Word."[94] This promise of adoption is found in the Scriptures, but its truth is realized through the inner witness of the Holy Spirit.

The other major aspect of Calvin's thought on adoption came from a covenantal dimension, which can be more easily understood today from a redemptive-historical theological perspective. More specifically, this refers to the unfolding of God's redemptive plan for mankind through his historical dealings with mankind. So when Calvin thinks of sonship in the Old Testament, he writes about it in New Testament terms. The covenant with Abraham was received by free adoption as sons by those who were formerly enemies (*Institutes* 1:10:1). The covenant with the Jews is referred to as a covenant of adoption (*Institutes* 3:2:22). Old Testament

---

92. Calvin, Institutes 4:17:2 and _Westhead, "Adoption in the Thought of John Calvin," 103–104.
93. Westhead, "Adoption in the Thought of John Calvin," 105.
94. Ibid., 105.

believers resembled slaves even though in fact they were sons. They were under guardianship until the time appointed by the Father, after which time they would be free. They were the corporate son of God and so were free, yet they did not possess that freedom until the coming of Christ.[95] This follows the thinking of Paul in Galatians 4, where the covenant by Hagar is a legal one, while that of Sarah is evangelical. One covenant made slaves, the other freemen. An inheritance is appointed for children, and since we are adopted as such, an inheritance has been ordained for us as well.[96]

Our future inheritance is the climax of our adoption, which includes the redemption of the body, without which the sacrifice and death of Christ would be in vain. The receipt of the heavenly inheritance and the redemption of the body becomes juxtaposed to a third and final element: all those he adopts he conforms to the image of Christ.[97] This is the climax of God's process of adoption—the image of God renewed in us. We become conformed not to the first Adam but to the last Adam, Jesus Christ.

Another aspect of Calvin's thought on adoption is that he viewed adoption and justification together. Adoption prior to the late eighteenth and mid-nineteenth centuries was not thought of as distinct from justification, much less as the ultimate goal of it, but rather as subordinate to it. According to Calvin, adoption is not a distinct locus of soteriology, but is a central core and privilege to those who are saved.[98] In Ephesians 1, Paul states that we were chosen in Christ before the foundation of the world to be holy and blameless; this predestination results in adoption as sons. Furthermore, this adoption results in an inheritance. Calvin sees God's free justification in Ephesians 1:6 in the word "acceptance." Our being destined to adoption further solidifies Calvin's position of equating justification and reconciliation, resulting in his thought that justification and adoption may as well not be seen as distinct.[99] *Institutes* 3:11:16 reads, "Christ cannot be torn into parts, so these two which we perceive in him conjointly are inseparable—namely, righteousness and sanctification. Whomever, therefore, God receives into grace, on them he at the same time bestows the Spirit of adoption (Rom 8:15)." Calvin's keeping justification and adoption together rather than viewing them separately may

---

95. Ibid., 110.
96. Calvin, *Commentary on the Epistle of Paul the Apostle to the Romans*, 301.
97. Westhead, "Adoption in the Thought of John Calvin," 111.
98. Kelly, McClure, and Rollinson, *The Westminster Confession of Faith*, 35.
99. Westhead, "Adoption in the Thought of John Calvin," 112.

have provided the grounds on which later theologians overlooked adoption to focus on sanctification.

The last aspect of Calvin's thoughts on the doctrine of adoption that I wish to discuss here are his views on adoption and the Christian life. Adoption consists of responsibilities and privileges that exist in the context of God's family. The adoptee has responsibilities toward the Father, the family, and finally the world. The first responsibility is to revere God as Father and act toward Him as sons (*Institutes* 3:11:6). Secondly, we are to show affection to our new family members and live in the reality that we now all have one Father (*Institutes* 3:20:36). The final responsibility is to live with a loving and forgiving spirit in our relationships to unbelievers. These are the marks of our adoption to the world.[100]

These weighty responsibilities could be viewed as burdens, but the privileges of adoption make them seem light. Through adoption we have confidence in our Father's care for us; in fact, He cares so much that he even pays attention to the number of hairs on our heads. Through adoption, we become sons and have hope beyond this world in our eternal inheritance. When God reveals Himself as Father, He testifies by His very self that we are His and that His mercy will never fail us. To look for help from any other source is to reproach God (*Institutes* 3:11:6).

In this world, the ideal advocate for anyone is his or her father. What greater comfort can we have than to have the God of all comfort and Father of all mercies for our security and defense! Our relationship to our Father gives us a new perspective from which to view all the hardships in the world. We come to understand that our Father of mercies is behind all our circumstances and uses them for our maturity and perfection (*Institutes* 3:8:1). "This is how even Christ as the Son of God learned obedience, and it is for the noble and ultimate purpose of conforming us to Christ's image that our Father so proceeds with us (Heb. 5:2)."[101]

From this short summary, we can see that the doctrine of adoption is peppered throughout Calvin's *Institutes* and other writings. Adoption was central to Calvin, as seen in the connection between adoption and the fatherhood of God, pneumatology, the covenant, justification, and the community of believers.[102] Calvin's thought closely mirrors that of Paul, and this explains his grasp of adoption. Calvin ties regeneration and adoption together in his commentary on the gospel of John:

---

100. Westhead, "Adoption in the Thought of John Calvin," 113

101. Ibid., 115.

102. Trumper, "The Metaphorical Import of Adoption: A Plea for Realisation," 140.

The enlightening of our minds by the Holy Spirit belongs to our renewal. So faith flows from its source, regeneration. But since by this same faith we receive Christ, who sanctifies us by His Spirit, it is called the beginning of our adoption. When the Lord breathes faith into us He regenerates us in a hidden and secret way that is unknown to us. But when faith has been given, we grasp with a lively awareness not only the grace of adoption but also newness of life and other gifts of the Holy Spirit.[103]

Additionally, in *Institutes* 3:3:10 we see that "the children of God [are] free through regeneration from the bondage of sin." But in this, we also see the uniqueness of adoption overlooked. Calvin mixes Pauline and Johannine terminology (regeneration versus bondage and freedom) without developing the differences. This suggests that Calvin may not have grasped the huiothesia as uniquely Pauline, or that he had realized it but had not worked out a clear way to connect adoption and regeneration without blurring the distinctiveness of either. The same can be said of later Puritan writings, whether those of the WCF or of theologians such as William Ames.[104]

Calvin's autobiographical account of his conversion informs us that his theology on adoption was not a mere abstraction, but radically affected his life. He believed he had no other hope or refuge for God's salvation other than His gracious adoption.[105] In the *Institutes*, he asserted that the authority of the gospel rests in adoption and how it empowers our salvation (*Institutes* 3:25:3). "It is a pity that, for whatever reason, his layout of the *Institutes* does not reflect the important place the doctrine of adoption occupies in his theology. That later Calvinism failed to pick up on this is in part due to Calvin's decision not to apportion the doctrine a section in the *Institutes*."[106]

---

103. Calvin, *The Gospel According to St. John*, 1–10, 19.
104. "In the biblical references added to the WCF, of twenty-one for the 'Adoption' chapter only nine come from Paul, four from the OT and eight from other NT books. It may be claimed without exaggeration that a perusal of post-Reformation reflections on adoption leads us to believe that John 1:12 is the closest rival to Galatians 4:4–5 as the *locus classicus* of adoption . . . In William Ames we have one such example. He lists 27 points under the heading of adoption. Of these 27 points, eight have no cross reference, six are supported by solely Pauline references . . . of the other fifteen three are supported exclusively by references to Hebrews and Revelation. Thus over half the points Ames makes are supported by texts written by authors who did not imply the adoption metaphor." From Trumper, "The Metaphorical Import of Adoption: A Plea for Realisation," 141.
105. "Life of John Calvin" (*Tracts*, vol. 1, cxxiv [CO 21 (49):162]), as cited by Tim Trumper in "The Theological History of Adoption I: An Account."
106. Trumper, "The Theological History of Adoption I: An Account," 20.

Chapter 6

Redeeming Samuel

By the beginning of 2011, things had begun to calm down for our family. Abigail was attaching well to our family and blossoming. Becky and I felt that our family wasn't complete quite yet, so we started to think out how to add to it yet again. We had briefly explored fertility options and realized they weren't for us, but we weren't ready for another struggle to adopt a child from the foster system. We heard through a mutual friend that a young mom had left her four-month-old son with a third party temporarily until a good home could be found for him, but that opportunity disappeared before we could act. So one night in April, at about ten o'clock, we decided to pray for another child. We prayed that the adoption would be easy and that God would make it clear that He was moving.

Less than a minute after we finished praying, the phone rang. It was the mutual friend. The first family for the little boy had given him back; were we interested? Of course! We were put in touch by phone with a family member of Amy's, the friend caring for Samuel. She worked out some details, and we went to meet him a day after the phone call. Amy's family wanted to meet us as well. We chatted for a while, and at the end of the conversation, we signed a power of attorney agreement. It was clearly stated in the agreement that the birth mom's intentions were to find Samuel a home and that we were now legally responsible for him. We went home with our new son that day. We thanked God for answering our prayer and began the process of getting the formal paperwork done.

During the intervening two weeks, I read two books: *Radical* by David Platt and *Crazy Love* by Francis Chan. I started to feel uneasy about how simple it had been to get Samuel. From what I gleaned from those books, I should expect such expressions of the gospel as adoption to be associated with struggle. I started to feel like we were going to need to contend for Samuel. Becky really didn't need to hear this—she now had three children on her hands and was trying to get ahold of Samuel's birth mom to finish up the adoption paperwork. The following day, Becky's birthday, we got a call from Amy: the birth mom wanted her son back as soon as possible. She had changed her mind. The struggle was about to begin.

The afternoon of that phone call, Becky drove to Amy's house and waited all afternoon for the birth mother, Karla, to come get Samuel, but she never showed. My wife left Samuel with Amy for several hours and then went late at night to bring him home when it was clear that his birth mother was not coming. We were relieved and thankful, but the same call came the following day, and Becky again went with Samuel to meet Karla. This time she showed up, and Becky gave Samuel to his birth mother. Becky also wrote her a letter, offering to be a resource and hoping to make a personal connection.

At this point we had no idea what to do. We had no legal standing, and yet we wanted to fight to give Samuel a home. We had fallen in love with this little boy, but we had no recourse. Becky kept in contact with Amy for a brief period of time and heard about how Samuel was back with Karla, but we also started to hear many disturbing and contradictory things about Amy and her situation from various sources. After two days, Amy stopped returning Becky's calls. For weeks my wife cried herself to sleep every night.

At this time we found out from another acquaintance that Karla had never left the house with Samuel—he had stayed with Amy. Amy had told Karla to ask for him back. She told Karla that we were bad people and that we were trying to steal Samuel. We also learned that the things Amy had told us about Karla were lies as well. We had been told that Karla wanted nothing to do with her son and that she was too busy doing drugs and prostituting herself to care about him. In reality, she did care for Samuel, but realizing her desperate situation and need for help, she had made the difficult decision to allow her friend to keep him. She did not realize that she had also been convinced to let her friend give her children to other families, and she did not remember signing any paperwork. So now we had no idea what to do or who to believe. The only things we knew were true were that we loved Samuel, wanted what was best for him, and had prayed and asked God for a baby, and He had answered that prayer. My wife kept repeating that God hadn't changed what He had told her—Samuel was to be our son.

So we prayed—a lot. We asked everyone we knew to pray for the situation. There were literally thousands of people around the world praying for him to be delivered from his circumstances. After two months, my wife felt that it was time to go to the county courthouse and petition for custody. It was a crazy idea. We had no legal standing and didn't even have physical custody—all we had was a lot of prayer and faith.

We were able to get an expedited court appearance due to safety issues in Amy's home, Amy's now-questionable psychological state, and the questionable activities going on where Samuel was living. Becky went to the courthouse to have the documents amended to allow her to appear as a party in the case for final determination of custody. We then learned that at one time prior to our involvement in this situation, Karla had felt uneasy with the arrangement and had also petitioned the court on behalf of Samuel; at the time she was supposed to appear in court about this, however, she was in the hospital due to a psychotic breakdown, and so she sent her "friend" Amy to vouch for her. Instead, Amy told the court that Karla was unfit, unstable, and a danger to her child. Amy requested and was granted legal custody at this hearing.

Throughout all of this, one of our prayers was that God would use even the evil done by others to bring about His good. We started to see this happening in a tangible way. The expedited county hearing was uneventful, but it did secure us legal standing and prompt a home evaluation by the county in which all of the possible placements for Samuel would be evaluated. The custody court hearing was going to occur one month later, and we had no idea what to expect. Then Karla reached out to Becky. She asked her to come to the upcoming court hearing because she now desired for us to gain custody of Samuel and did not want him to stay with her friend any longer. She had started to get some clarity into what was going on, and we were the only people she knew with the resources and the desire to help him. We have no idea how she reached that clarity or what transpired to help her see all the lies (her psychiatric illness makes it hard for her to have perspective and insight at times). Whatever happened, it was glorious: she was now fighting for her son to have a home! It was painful to see Karla so torn as to whom to believe and then to trust in a friend who wished her only harm.

During that month, though Karla initially had the clarity of mind to realize all that was going on, she later began to feel that maybe it would be better for Samuel to stay with Amy after all. By the day of court, she had completely changed her mind again. Amy had her four-year-old son as well, and Karla was so desperate to keep contact with him that she again started to believe Amy despite everything that had transpired. We walked into the court hearing knowing that we cared deeply for Karla, seeing that she was being manipulated, but not having any idea whether this would be made clear or whether the court would be able to determine the truth amidst all of the confusion.

Through all this chaos, a miracle happened. The judge saw things for what they were and awarded us physical custody, with shared joint custody with Karla and Samuel's birth father. In the following months, Becky had many conversations with Karla. Throughout this whole process, Becky came to love her and see how much grace God had shown her. Even though Karla has none of her four biological children, all but one is in a Christian home and flourishing. Karla sees this as God's grace and knows that it is unusual, though she hasn't yet grasped that this is a sign of God's grace to her specifically and not just to her children.

At the final custody hearing, a strange thing happened: the birth father showed up in court. We had never seen him, and he had never attempted to contact us. In the final decision, the judge added him to the custody agreement and gave Amy visiting rights. A very weird situation indeed. As I write this, that was ten months ago. We haven't heard anything from the birth father, and Amy doesn't return any of Becky's calls.

Becky threw Samuel a birthday party five months after we got him back and invited everyone. Amy showed up as well as Karla. What we've seen through this whole process is a clear demonstration of God's grace and providence. He doesn't work according to our ways, but with a higher good in view. We know he is the Father of the fatherless and that His ultimate goal is the physical and spiritual redemption of Samuel. God also has a heart for the birth mothers who either voluntarily or involuntarily give up their children. Many times they are fatherless themselves and need a home and family just as their children do. We had never thought of this aspect of orphan care before, but we were compelled to do so because of Samuel's circumstances. We regularly meet with Karla, and she texts Becky often to tell her that she loves her. Through our unconditional and radical love of her son, she has seen a glimpse of the kind of love the Father has for her. This whole process has brought her closer to knowing God and seeing what a family looks like. In many ways we consider her as part of our family, and our daughters love to see her and call her Auntie Karla.

We are excited to see how God is going to work this whole situation out for His glory, even though we have no idea what it's going to look like in the end. Whether the legal situation remains unchanged for years to come or we have the opportunity for an open adoption, we have had to become comfortable with uncertainty in our new "extended" family. We are becoming more at ease with this bizarre situation, knowing that it will work out for our good and God's glory. This has been a hard process for our family, but a redeeming process as well, and those around us have been able to see God working through this over the last eighteen months. The process of "redeeming Samuel" has opened our hearts not only to him, but to Karla and even Amy. We have come to realize that God has an unending love for all the fatherless and defenseless, not just cute little babies in foreign countries. There is a huge unmet need here in my city, and in yours, that God wants His church to meet. Sin blinds, scars, and deceives, but God can and does use even it to His glory.

Chapter 7

Adoption and Understanding
Our Religious Experience

My theological studies of adoption were prompted by and enriched by my experience of adopting children. And as theology and practice have so powerfully met, they have given me a deep understanding of my own religious experience of adoption, with its privileges and obligations. This treasure is for the whole church. Up to this point, we have been discussing the individual aspects of the doctrine of adoption. In this chapter, I would like to briefly summarize these findings and then relate how they are important to our understanding of Scripture holistically and the resulting implications in the life of the church.

A Redemptive Historical Summary of the Doctrine of Adoption

God's divine election from before the foundation of the world included our adoption in Christ. God condescended to man and started to display this plan by setting His heart on Israel. While the Israelites were slaves in Egypt, God called them "my son" and began the task of redeeming them to Himself. After rescuing the Israelites with a strong arm, He brought them to His holy mount and gave them His Law. Part of this Law and the rules in it were to remind the Israelites of where they had come from and their identity prior to their rescue. For this reason, very specific laws were given to regulate care for the orphan or fatherless. Strong judgment was handed out if the Israelites did not care for the powerless and the weak, for God identified Himself as their Father.

Israel disobeyed God's Law and fell back into bondage and slavery, but God never gave up on His son, nor did He forget His covenant with Abraham. God's divine decree was that His only begotten Son would come to redeem His people, but at the level of the individual. Each would become a partaker of the Holy Spirit, who would seal or secure everyone in adoption, never to be lost again. While on earth, the only begotten Son made a special effort to associate with the disenfranchised and equated care for them for caring for Him. He showed the spiritual significance of His mercy in parables and stories. In Matthew 18, He tells a story in which a master forgives an unrepayable debt and expects that servant, in a similar fashion but to a lesser degree, to forgive others. And in Matthew 25 He tells how, when He returns, He will judge based on how the righteous cared for "the least of these."

Paul expounded the significance of our adoption in Christ, how it changes all our relationships and how we are now to interact with the world around us. James showed the practical aspect of what this means and how care for the widow and orphan is an essential aspect of true religion. James' call alludes to God's call to His people to do justice and mercy. This is seen in Micah 6:8 and other places in the Law where God directly equates His mercy to His people with how they show mercy to the weak and helpless around them.

The underlying theme of all this is that God has redeemed Israel from slavery and adopted them into His family, and that He has a special place in His heart for the downcast, forsaken, and above all the fatherless. For this reason he structured the Law to protect this group and commanded His people to carry out that protection. In the New Testament, we discover that we have been grafted into the family of God in a unique way that was hidden from the prophets of old. This adoption into God's family heightens the Law in its spiritual meaning and significance, and it should equally heighten our concern for the orphan. We too were once orphans in this world, and as those redeemed from the curse of the Law, we should mirror the act of God in our lives in a tangible way through care and protection of the orphan.

We have been adopted in Christ. We have been redeemed. We have been rescued from slavery and made free in the family of God. These are historical realities of God's moving on our behalf. The next logical step is for us to mirror in this world what God has done for us in this life and the eternal life to come. Though ours must be a poor and meagerly image of His immeasurable work, it will show the world in a demonstrative way what the Father has done for us. But more importantly, orphan care is an Old Testament mandate that has been expanded in the New Testament.

The Doctrine of Adoption and the World Around Us

Our religious experience of being brought into the family of God, receiving a new family, a new name, and an eternal inheritance, occurs through our spiritual adoption. Understanding this changes how we understand and experience our salvation and redemption. When Paul wrote

Romans, he knew his audience well and wanted them to understand how radical their adoption into the family of God by the faith of Abraham truly was. He was writing to a Jewish community in a Hellenistic world under Roman law. In this culture, unwanted children were routinely sold into slavery, abandoned, or exposed. In some cases, poor parents might allow their child to be adopted by a wealthier couple. Roman culture placed a high value on succession and producing heirs, so a childless couple would be eager to adopt. The Roman law provided that an adopted child had all the rights of inheritance that belonged to biological children.[107]

Paul assures his readers in Romans 8 that God has not left them alone or abandoned them in their struggle in this world, but has claimed them as His very own children and inheritance. Though they are in the midst of a severe persecution and struggle, they should be assured of their status as adopted children in Christ and not doubt their future inheritance as God's beloved children. Paul uses the adoption metaphor again in Galatians 4 to reassure his readers that their status is not a lesser status than that of natural Jews, but that they hold the same status in the family as those natural-born.

As those adopted through Christ, we, like the Romans and Galatians, are in a great struggle, experiencing longing for that which is yet not fully complete. How can that be? In Romans 7 and 8, Paul shows his readers that the suffering and longing they experience is not proof of their separation from Him, but rather evidence of their belonging to Him. The indwelling Holy Spirit is at odds with the condition of the world and longs for the banishment of sin and death. As joint heirs with Christ, we expect to share in His sufferings as well as His glory. The world too is in this state of tension. It groans in expectation of the manifestation of the sons of God, knowing that it will be renewed at their revelation (Romans 8:16–24).

We groan within ourselves in solidarity with creation for this manifestation. "Believers are being saved not from creation but with creation . . . Having the Spirit does not distance believers from creation but increases the solidarity of believers with creation."[108] However, even as the Spirit groans within us, we have hope—this Spirit has been given us as a pledge of the life to come. It is a sign of our redemption. This seal of our adoption, though not complete, gives us hope that He who has begun a good work will complete it in the end (Philippians 1:6).

---

107. Koester, History, *Culture and Religion of the Hellenistic Age*, 65.
108. Dunn, "Spirit Speech: Reflections on Romans 8:12–27," 84.

We have been sealed, the legal adoption papers have been signed, yet we do not reside with our heavenly Father. We struggle and hurt; at times we feel abandoned; and at others we feel His love. The tension of belonging to God, yet still living in this broken world, estranged from our true home in heaven, at times seems unbearable and incomprehensible. "Far from promising a life free of grief and pain, our adoption as God's children means that we will share in the sufferings of Christ for the sake of God's good purposes, for the liberation of a world in bondage," in order that God may be all and in all when God's redemptive plan finally is complete.[109] We have become a part of God's eternal plan for the redemption of the world, and this creates a tension and expectation within the believer.

And yet we long for others to be adopted just as we are in order to one day experience the union with Christ that we so desperately long for. This is where the paradigm of spiritual adoption and its struggle meets that of natural adoption in this world. It is moving to see the pain and suffering of couples struggling to adopt a child. Regardless of the setbacks, they remain steadfast in the face of what at times appear to be insurmountable obstacles and defeats. There seems to be no limit to what they will do in order to complete the adoption and make that child their own. "Is this not an apt metaphor for what God has done for us in Christ, expending himself in order to make us who are 'orphans' in a world of sin and death his very own children and heirs? Is this not a poignant image of the God who pursues us relentlessly until our adoption is complete and will not let us go?"[110]

Adoption is the clearest example on earth of unearned acceptance and love by another family, bestowing a new status and name that is unrelated to the previous one. It is a clear and poignant declaration of the gospel. The worse the birth situation and circumstances are, the greater the grace and mercy shown to the adoptee, and correspondingly, the greater the love displayed. Our response to orphans and their need for care offers us as the church a unique opportunity to show what true fatherhood is and instill lifelong positive constructs in the adoptee, the new family, our church families, and the communities in which they exist. It is unfortunate that at times one result of adoption in our fallen world is that adoptees face intra- and interpersonal struggles and a sense of low self-worth—indeed, it should be that because of their adoption, they hold a sense of their

---

109. Johnson, "Waiting for Adoption: Reflections on Romans 8:12–25," 312.
110. Ibid., 311.

uniqueness and special worth as those chosen through no works or characteristics of their own! Because they are made in God's image, they have value and countless worth.

The ultimate struggle we all face is the struggle with the understanding of God, "the fundamental symbol of our ultimate concern."[111] Struggling with our apparent losses in the context of that concern creates a depth, direction, and unity to all our lesser concerns, resulting in a deepening of the whole person. The crisis that adoptees face is one of true identity and lineage. Biologically, they are from one family, but relationally and emotionally, they are from another. "Escaping God, refusing to notice our own nakedness, is always the temptation."[112] "When God is not apprehended because spiritual suffering leaves one blind to God's being in early life, the very resource that is needed for spiritual imagination and refreshment is not available. This is sometimes the dilemma of the adoptee—the real God is not experienced as being around."[113] Yet He has decreed that they be redeemed out of their birth situations and placed into new families which choose them, not because of where they have come from but *despite* where they have come from. This clear representation of the gospel in their earthly redemption should point adoptees to their heavenly Father and His desire for their eternal redemption—and it should point all the rest of us there as well.

Ultimately, the adoptee's struggle is not unique. This struggle of identity and belonging is the struggle of every believer prior to coming into the family of God. We were all estranged from God. We were all at one time strangers to Him and His love. We were slaves to sin and bound to iniquity. In fact, we were His enemies and at war against the only one who has ever loved us perfectly. We were at enmity with the Father of Lights. Our sins were the reason His Son had to go to the cross. We didn't sense His presence, though there has never been a time in which He was not near; and we didn't sense His love, though His love has always been poured out to us.

All of mankind struggles with a sense of estrangement from our true nature. We are separated from our truest identity, found in unbroken relationship with God our Father, Maker, and Redeemer, and so we struggle to find a sense of meaning. Unfortunately, this is usually done outside of God. We attempt to maintain this separation psychologically, and so our

---

111. Tillich, *The Courage to Be*, 4–5.
112. Nydam, "Adoption and the Image of God," 257.
113. Ibid. 257.

minds set up an unending host of idols in order to escape the reality of God as Maker and Redeemer. For the Christian, turning to God means taking on a true identity in Christ which is outside the ability of the world to apprehend. This sense of identity is essential for us to stand up in the world as persons who are part of a redeemed community. This identity begins in our awareness of our personal past (which includes our ethnic and cultural identities) put in the context of what our new future holds in the family of God. Our pilgrimage on earth creates the inner tension of the already and the not yet. We know where God has brought us from, and we wait expectantly for the completion of where he is going to take us.

"Religious experience is the experience of struggling with being it-self."[114] Understanding all of this, we can grasp the possibility for a deeper understanding of God that an adopted individual has. Adoptees uniquely are strangers and pilgrims in this world, abandoned by their genetic fami-lies. They are uniquely chosen in this world, both by an adopted family and by God Himself, who placed them in their new homes. The danger is that they will falter psychologically and be unable to comprehend what true family is, thus developing a psychological illness, such as depression or another malady. But the potential is also there that, unlike anyone else, they will grasp the deeper meaning of adoption by God through their per-sonal experience, and through their understanding and experience, will teach the unadopted the deeper meaning of the fatherhood of God.

There also is an opportunity for the church to better understand grace through the understanding of the adoptee. Many people struggle with a sense of self-worth and a lack of meaningful familial ties, resulting in an inability to apprehend the reality of God as Father. The power to affirm one's self is a gift, not an ability or a mere act. Said another way, "This is not a pulling-of-bootstraps activity, not a work, not an accomplishment, but instead the moment of meeting and knowing the God beyond God in the midst of diminishment and shame."[115] It is a matter of grace. Adoptees understand this experientially like no one else. Their experience is not just spiritual, but emotional and physical. Their struggle is deeper and more palpable than what others will face, but their struggle also gives them the opportunity to understand the heights of God's grace in a way that others cannot. Adoptees experience the joy of being chosen by a set of parents and placed in a home. They have to deal with the emotions and trials that

---

114. Nydam, "Adoption and the Image of God," 259.
115. Ibid., 258.

stem from their initial abandonment, yet they also recognize the mercy, grace, and favor associated with another placing their love on them. They have to intellectually and emotionally tackle the hardships that stem from the previous life in the context of a new life and family. Unadopted Christians many times do not grasp the spiritual implications of their new family in light of the old, nor of their new relationship and obligations in light of their old life. The adoptee has a greater capacity to apprehend the implications of their vertical adoption because they also have had a horizontal adoption. Like the prodigal son who "came to himself," and the modern Christian who "experiences God," the adoptee has both a physical coming home and a spiritual awakening.

The doctrine of adoption, expressed in the physical world through the acts of adopting and orphan care, offers us an opportunity to understand our position in the family of God better, and then to show the world an example of what it looks like to be in God's family. Through the doctrine of adoption, we comprehend what God has done. Through the care of the orphan, we mirror what He has done, and through preaching, we tell of what He has done. Reclaiming adoption in the life of the church and in our personal lives would radically transform the church and make it conform that much more to the image of Christ, enabling it to more fully display His image in this world.

Chapter 8

Hindrances to Adoption

The theological doctrine of adoption, which we have been exploring in depth up to this point, has major ramifications for our lives in this world. Starting in this chapter, we will change gears and start to look at sociological adoption and its place in the Christian life. When most people think about orphan care, their thoughts automatically gravitate to the adoption of children—but caring for the fatherless is much more than that. This section will expand the doctrine of adoption through demonstrating the need for sociological adoption, the adoption of children, and orphan care, and then discuss why these things don't often happen in the church relative to their theological importance in Scripture.

The population explosion of the twentieth century has been accompanied by an explosion in the number of orphans. In 2006, there were 143,400,000 orphans in the world.[116] This number translates to one in thirteen children in the developed world. This is a steep rise from the UNICEF numbers released in 2002, in which there were 70,000,000 orphans in the world, or roughly one in twenty.[117] More than 16 million were orphaned in 2003, and to date, over 15 million children have been orphaned by AIDS.[118] The sheer need for orphan care is greater now than at any other time in history. So why, as a whole, is caring for the orphan off the radar of most churches and most Christians?

There are several ways to understand the lack of church involvement in addressing this need. The first is our culture's philosophical bent away from adoption, which is expressed in "genealogical essentialism."[119] This philosophy was seen in our friend Sandy's reaction to adoption, as I shared it at the beginning of this book: it is a core belief that is expressed in the idea that the only "real" family is a genealogical family, one in which children share the genetic makeup of their parents. In the past, this was understood in terms of blood kinship.

---

116. UNICEF, *The State of the World's Children 2006*, 113.
117. Davis, *Fields of the Fatherless*, 38.
118. UNICEF, "Who Are the Invisible?"
119. Post, "Adoption Theologically Considered," 150.

As evolutionary theory has become embedded in our collective psyche, genetic makeup has become more pivotal to our self-identity. Scientific developments such as in vitro fertilization (IVF) and intracyto-plasmic sperm insemination (ICSI) have helped to propagate this thinking to a new level. Human DNA has been described as fundamental to human identity and fate. As more research into human genetics comes to the forefront, scientists are accounting more human characteristics and disease processes to our genetic makeup. In the medical field, the result is a stronger emphasis on the genetic basis of disease. In the societal arena, this is lending scientific support to a general anti-adoption sentiment in our society.

At the most basic level, this prejudice is expressed in our concept of "real" parents. The real parents are the sperm and egg donors who give us our genetic material, not the persons who care, nurture, and provide for us for the first eighteen-plus years of our life. This is in opposition to the biblical view, which challenges our cultural assumptions that only birth kinship is "real" kinship. One unfortunate practical result of this is that when Christian couples are faced with infertility, they lean more toward IVF or other fertility treatments than adoption. If their views were influenced by the doctrine of adoption, sociological adoption would be the first thing they would think of, not scientific procedures. For those made in the image of God, adopted into the family of God, and called on by God to defend the fatherless, imaging Him in this world through natural adoption or orphan care would seem to be the natural response. "Even if blood is thicker than water, it is not thicker than *agape* . . . Families can be built as well as they can be begotten."[120] We must remember that families can be created by agape as well as begotten biologically; this is how the first family can into being.[121]

A natural assumption that arises from our cultural bent against adoption is the commonly held belief that adopted children are more likely to suffer from mental disease and family discord. It only seems natural that adoptive families would be less stable, but a recent study on adoption showed that to the contrary, adoption creates a more stable home environment, and adoptive children are at least as psychologically stable as their

---

120. Post, "Adoption Theologically Considered," 151.
121. There is not space to further develop this idea, but Scripture is clear in the New Testament, and the doctrine was further developed by Calvin, that the love between the Father, Son, and Holy Spirit was the driving force for the creation of man in God's image.

non-adopted counterparts. This study of 715 randomly selected families between 1974 to 1980 looked at adopted children ages twelve to eighteen. [122] Some of their findings are as follows:

- Adoptive families have considerably lower divorce rates compared to non-adoptive families.
- Adopted children have slightly better psychological health compared to their non-adopted peers.
- The self-esteem of adopted children is similar to that of their non-adopted peers.
- The majority of adopted children accept their adoption with ease; only 27 percent see adoption as problematic in how they view themselves.
- Adopted children are as deeply connected to their adopted parents as their non-adopted siblings.

Another hindrance to adoption and orphan care has been their lack of development in modern Christian ethics, except in a narrow spectrum as a response to abortion. It is difficult to discuss Christian ethics as they relate to adoption due to the lack of literature to review! The only active substantial ethical discussions on adoption in the church world today are as it relates to combating abortion. [123] Abortion is a divisive topic in our culture and churches. Limiting the ethical discussion of orphan care in this way has only served to limit the discussion without aiding the pro-life cause.

The third and most important hindrance to sociological adoption in the church is the lack of its theological development and exposition by church leaders. "Theology is the application of the Word of God by persons to all areas of life." [124] One of the major goals of this work is to show the lack of development of the doctrine of adoption despite its importance and prevalence throughout Scripture. The theological underdevelopment of the doctrine of adoption in the church has naturally resulted in a paucity of its practice by the church. Seminary students don't systematically study our adoption in Christ. The result is that adoption isn't preached from the pulpit or discussed in the pews. It is not mentioned in premarital counseling as a gospel-centered response to infertility, even though

---

122. Benson, Sharma, and Roehlkepartain, *Growing Up Adopted*, 1984.
123. Post, "Adoption Theologically Considered," 150.
124. Frame, *The Doctrine of the Knowledge of God*, 81.

roughly 20 percent of women will experience fertility issues.[125] This is a huge struggle for many, yet I have never spoken with a married couple who received any premarital counseling from their pastors about infertility and how it relates to adoption.

Christian laypersons aren't taught to think of themselves as adoptees in the family of God. James 1:27 defines true religion in terms of orphan and widow care, yet we don't think of ourselves or our churches in those terms. God the Father calls Himself the Father of the fatherless, yet as those created in His image, we don't struggle with what that means practically in our lives and church communities. If we saw ourselves as those redeemed from this world through adoption into the family of God, and if we understood the New Testament message of adoption through propitiation in the context of the knowledge that we are made in God's image and called to do the same works as our Father, it would result in a culture of adoption and orphan care within the church (John 5:36, 14:10–12).[126]

The last hindrance to adoption is adoption itself. Adoption is an expression of the gospel. Care of the orphan is a part of our biblical mandate on earth. Without our understanding the theological aspect of adoption, it becomes mere charity, and without our practicing the missional aspect, it becomes mere metaphor. If we believe Jesus about heavenly things—our adoption in Christ—we will mirror Him in earthly things—the adoption and care of children. But adoption is warfare. It is contested in its theological, missional, and cosmic aspects. Anyone who has adopted can attest to the mental, emotional, and spiritual battle experienced in rescuing an orphan. The battle Satan wages seems to converge on orphans whom God later uses in His plan to rescue His people (i.e., Moses and Jesus). In the end, it's an adopted babe in a manger who sets the captives free and breaks open the gates of hell. The Scriptures inform us that there are powers that would rather we not know our identity in Christ, that would rather we ignore the earthly type and shadow of our heavenly reality to find our identity in what we can see and identify with our senses.

The satanic powers want to rule the universe, but a tiny baby born in a manger has conquered their reign. Thus, they rage all the more against babies made in His image. This titanic warfare is imaged in Revelation 12. A woman is about to bear a man-child who will rule the nations with a rod

---

125. "Fertility, Family Planning, and Reproductive Health of U.S. Women," Centers for Disease Control and Prevention, www.cdc.gov/nchs/fastats/fertile.htm.
126. Packer, *Knowing God*, 214.

of iron, and the dragon awaits His birth to consume Him, but He is caught up to heaven. The dragon then goes out to make war with the children of the woman, and he has done so ever since.

The battle against babes is a story that has played out from the beginning in Scripture. This makes sense given the fact of who, in the end, was to enter the world to bring down its principalities and powers. Cain, the seed of the Evil One, murders righteous Abel (1 John 3:12); Pharaoh orders the murder of the innocents (Exodus 1 and 2); Herod does the same in Bethlehem in hopes of murdering Jesus (Matthew 2:16). In the ancient world, infanticide was a common occurrence, and there was a low value on human life as a whole.[127] There was even a demon-god in the Old Testament, called Molech, who demanded the sacrifice of infants to satiate his wrath. God forbade Israel from his worship and even threatened punishment on those who turns away from punishing one who gave his child to Molech (Leviticus 20:4–5).

Children, and especially orphans, have a special place in God's heart. He redeems us to Himself through the Spirit by adoption, effected in the blood of His Son. For us to image God in this world through adoption will be battle. "The demonic powers hate babies because they hate Jesus . . . They know the human race is saved—and they are vanquished—by a woman giving birth (Gal. 4:4; 1 Tim 2:15)."[128] What if Christians were once again known as those who care for orphans and the church reclaimed its role in defending the fatherless? "Adoption is about an entire culture within our churches, a culture that sees adoption as part of our Great Commission mandate and as a sign of the gospel itself."[129]

We should also realize that part of our final judgment at the coming of the kingdom of God will arise from our care of the orphan. If it is one of the three pillars of true religion, we should expect no less. In Matthew 25, Jesus states that the sheep and the goats will be judged based on their treatment of the hungry, naked, and homeless. Job realized this over a thousand years prior and stated it in Job 31. In his defense against his friends accusations, Job says that he has been the champion of the widow from the time he left the womb, and from his youth he has been a father to the fatherless. In this passage, Job's main defense against his accusers is the fact that he defended the least of these. God has given Himself the

---

127. Schmidt, *How Christianity Changed the World*, 48–75.
128. Moore, *Adopted for Life*, 64.
129. Ibid., 19.

title Father of the fatherless and has entrusted us to carry out their care on His behalf here on earth (Psalm 68:5, Exodus 22:22–24, Deuteronomy 14:29). Not to do so is to miss one of the major pillars of mercy in the Old Testament and one of the pillars of true religion in the New.

As a man thinks, so is he (Proverbs 23:7). Of all the hindrances above, the most fundamental is the theological. If we understand more clearly what God has done for us, we will be better informed in what we do for our fellow man. We can only know ourselves by knowing God, and in knowing Him, we will come to think His thoughts. We will love what He loves and hate what He hates. We will be angry when He is angry and have pity when He has pity. We will have His mercy in our lives and be the defenders, protectors, and guides to the fatherless. We can be no less; He has commanded us to do so.[130]

---

130. Deuteronomy 10:18, 24:17, 26:13, 27:19; Isaiah 1:17,23, 10:2; Jeremiah 49:11.

Chapter 9

A Gospel-Centered, Grace-Driven
Life and Family

Leading a gospel-centered, grace-driven life will look different for every individual and family. My wife and I are slowly starting to see what this means for our family, and it is changing what our family looks like. But at the most basic level, leading a gospel-centered, grace-driven life means that, based on the good news of Christ's coming and redeeming us, a change occurs in our lives that is in response to God's work and that is empowered by His grace. It will make our lives and families look different and set us apart from those around us. As the gospel is more deeply explored, its significance to us will expand, and our grace-filled response will become more potent.

Gospel simply means "good news." The Scriptures expound what this good news is and what it means for our lives. Yes, God came to save the lost, and it did cost Him. But the gospel is so much more. God the Father planned our redemption from sin before time began and the worlds were formed. At the center of His plan was that His only begotten Son would have to leave His side and suffer death on the cross to redeem us at an immeasurable cost to both Father and Son. The focus of history would become the redemption of His people.

A grace-driven response is ultimately based on the identity of God. Because of who He is and what He does, He redeems us. As we realize the enormity of what God has done and to what great lengths He has gone to save us, we are driven to respond. Because it is of grace, it is unmerited, and we can never work enough to earn God's favor. Yet at the same time we are freed to serve Him without fear, knowing that our response is acceptable to Him by faith through the work of His Son. We are freed to serve God with all our heart, mind, soul, and strength, regardless of the results of our service, knowing we are already accepted in the beloved.

Personal Disclosure

When we started this journey of adoption six years ago, we had no idea what it was that we were doing—we only were responding to our very basic understanding of the gospel. Because of what God has done for us, as those made in His image, we should attempt to mirror Him and His work here on earth. This will mean different things for different families and individuals. For us, it has meant adopting all of our children from desperate situations and spending our energy to make them ours. Our family looks different to all around us. When we are in public, it is obvious to all that we have adopted. My children have unique needs due to their birth histories, and it has been—and continues to be—a struggle to meet those needs. Yet I wouldn't have it any other way. Our decisions to follow God's leading in this area have cost us an enormous amount of time, money, energy, and emotional capital, yet my wife and I wouldn't change a thing. We have been changed through following God in the area of adoption. We have chosen each one of our children, and I want them to grow up knowing that. In fact, one of the main reasons I started this book was so that when my children are older, they will have something to read that helps them understand what their adoption means and to see how very special they are.

Following God from a gospel-centered, grace-driven perspective has changed how Becky and I respond to struggles in life and especially to our struggle with infertility. We had been married for two years in 2006 and had been trying to get pregnant for some time. We had both contemplated adoption, but on our own terms. Unknown to me, Becky had already fallen in love with Anna, one of her patients. She had been working with Anna from the day she left the hospital, and her foster home would soon be closing. I was open to adoption, but only because of my basic understanding of James 1:27. After we had Anna, we started to think about fertility treatments but decided that at that time, they weren't for our family. Almost immediately thereafter, the opportunity to adopt Abigail arose. A year after we adopted her, we investigated further our options, including IVF, ICSI, and even embryo adoption. All were very expensive options but in many ways would be easier than the struggle of adopting out of foster care.

Finally, we went to a fertility specialist to discuss embryo adoption, which led us to a conversation about ICSI. Honestly, we were both tired of fighting to get our children, and we wanted to take an easier route. It was only then that we found out the cause of our fertility issues. I have a chromosomal defect, making it impossible for me to have children or to consider any fertility technology options.

In retrospect, our response was very telling. Neither of us got upset or emotional. My ego and masculinity were not affected. I didn't feel like

I was any less of a man, nor did my wife feel hurt that she would never be able to be pregnant and carry my child. In a real and palpable way, I can say that sin has marred me spiritually, physically, and even genetically. But God's transforming work has been just as real. Our response to this discovery was simple: "So, now where do we adopt from?" Our response would have been drastically different had we learned this four years previously.

We started to pray about where to go from there, and less than two months later we got involved with Samuel and our greatest struggle yet to adopt a child. God was just preparing us for the next stage in the saga. Even one year before, I would have never ventured into a situation like we are in now. I wouldn't have put myself in a situation full of deceit and lies to the point of being accused in court of extortion. I wouldn't have been willing to continue to reach out to Karla and Amy. I wouldn't have allowed my family to get intertwined with these dysfunctional families. But most importantly, I wouldn't have been willing to extend myself at great cost and injury to redeem Samuel and give him a home. It's awesome to look back and see how God has been preparing us at every stage of our journey for the next. It has always been a struggle; it has always been hard. But living this gospel-centered life has allowed God's plan for Samuel's earthly redemption to include me and my family. It has always required us to sacrifice something we told ourselves we would never sacrifice. It continues to push us to new heights of compassion and care for Karla. And it continues to display the grace of God through the gospel in our lives in continually deeper ways.

A Birth Mother's Story; An Adoptive Mother's Struggle

Karla is not the only birth mother we have maintained a relationship with. We are also in touch with Anna's mother, Tammy, and Becky has invested a great deal in her life. To end this chapter, I want to turn to my wife and to Tammy and to let them speak, illuminating this process and the difference the gospel makes not only in the lives of adopted children, but also of others who are equally "fatherless."

* * *

Journal Entry: Monday, November 5, 2007
I talked to my child's birth mother again today. Such a strange relationship. I had heard of "open adoption," and as much as I knew I would love to

adopt someday, I didn't think that would be the way I would go. But sometimes God just has another plan in mind.

We first met over the phone when I asked Anna's caseworker to pass along my phone number in hopes that it would help Birth Mom make the decision to let us take Anna into our home. It went well. She gave her permission for us to have Anna live with us.

We talked again a little while later, and she informed me that she had left California and was back in Florida, and could she see Anna as soon as possible? That night our closest friends here threw a "Welcome Anna" surprise party to celebrate her being with us (not knowing that her mom had come back). So we all prayed; it was part of the plan.

After that, Birth Mom and I met in court on several occasions. It was a little strange, but we actually kind of talked like friends. She respected the fact that I was taking care of her daughter, and I wanted her to know that I loved the opportunity to do so—and that I loved her daughter.

Then came the day when Birth Mom thought she was ready to give us her blessing and would go ahead and sign parental right surrenders instead of going to trial with the case. She came right up to me that day when I got there and said, "You want her, don't you?" I told her the truth, and she wasn't threatened by it. But the court system did not see fit to let it happen that day. Or a month later.

Our relationship, however, grew each time we saw one another. I took the position that the past is the past and none of us can do anything to change it. No judgment.

On September 27, 2007, Birth Mom was finally able to surrender her legal rights. She did so heroically. That is, until she turned around and looked at me and saw that I was crying as I watched the whole process unfold. Then we were both crying. It was one of the great privileges of my life to observe that kind of love; she was finally able to make a decision that was totally selfless on her child's behalf. On my child's behalf.

She hugged me and cried and told me she loves me. She says that every time we talk. And I say it back.

My name is Rebekah Hartman. As I sit to write this, that relationship with Anna's birth mother has grown still. Five years ago, I prayed and dreamed that maybe when our kids were grown, we'd be able to sit and talk openly with their birth parents and allow a relationship to develop out of that. I don't know if I thought it would happen for sure, but I definitely believed the possibility existed. Little did I know that such a very short while later, we'd have already been given the incredible gift of those prayers being answered and that dream becoming reality.

When we read in the Bible that we are to care for orphans and widows, we rarely include the fatherless mom in the midst of a crisis pregnancy or the mother addicted to drugs who is struggling to care for her children. They were made in the image of God, and often, they are also fatherless. We are awakening to the needs to multitudes of children needing families, but we often forsake the mothers. Our journey finally led us to a point where we began to wonder how we can read God's words about the orphan, the widow, and the stranger and not recognize that those words in no way limit the scope of our responsibility to adorable infants or very young children in need of families. There are single mothers in need of support, teenage children who may already have children themselves and are desperate for families, and birth parents who desire for their children all of the things they are unable to provide, but who deeply desire that someone would look at them and realize that they too are in need of all those things—that someone might look at them and recognize their infinite worth and value.

Tammy and I hope that by sharing a part of our story, from a birth mother and an adoptive mother, we can encourage others and the gospel can shine forth as two broken people share how God has written an amazing story simply because we put one foot in front of the other and allowed Him to open our hearts to one another.

Here is Tammy's story as she shared it with me:

> All my life, I had a father, but that relationship was nowhere near what I think it was supposed to be. I didn't know my biological dad, and the dad who raised me did not love me the way a father should love his child. Life beat me down, and then I beat myself down even more. In some ways, I never would've imagined my life being the way that it is, and in another it's hard to believe that I didn't begin using drugs sooner.
>
> When I became pregnant, I was ashamed of myself, and I really didn't see my future. I was unsure, scared. The bigger part of me wanted to think that I would get better and get clean and be her mom, but I just didn't see that happening. I alienated myself; it was just me, alone in a trailer with no power or water,

and if I ate an orange or a pack of crackers in a day, I was lucky. I had no hope. Everyone wanted to tell me what I should do. I thought about terminating the pregnancy, and then I thought the drugs would probably take care of things even if I didn't have an abortion. I was concerned for the child growing inside me and felt guilt for abandoning my older daughter as well. I never felt like God abandoned me, but like I had left Him and couldn't be close to Him because of my choices. I also doubted and was unsure about God because my family had such different views and thoughts about Him, it was confusing to me to know what to believe.

The day my water broke and I realized my child was coming, I waited twenty-four hours to get to the hospital since that was when I could get someone to pick me up and take me. I knew before I even left the house that my daughter wouldn't come home with me. I was hoping that if I waited, maybe the drugs would be clear of my system, but I was also scared to death of what that would mean for her. They gave me a strong sedative at the hospital because I was out of my head and filled with shame and fear for what was about to happen. I woke up hours later screaming with pain, got an epidural, and the next thing I remember was them telling me that my daughter was here and that she would not be able to come home with me. I was so ashamed I didn't even want to go see her.

After Anna was in foster care for a few months, I made the decision to leave the state because I wanted to get clean and get myself straight. I couldn't do it if I stayed there because there would always be someone showing up at the door ready to drag me back down. I had been told that as long as I did the classes and everything that was required to get my daughter back, they would be counted, but it would be harder and take a lot longer from out of state. I felt like a horrible person and was overwhelmed with guilt, like I was cheating her to be away from her. I didn't know if my choices had caused her health issues and premature birth. I was in denial of the whole situation until just before her first birthday when I finally confronted the fact that she had cerebral palsy. The shame hit even harder because I thought maybe my choices caused her disability. At that point, I didn't see myself as a worthwhile person, even though deep down I did know I had worth.

I did get clean, and I returned to the state to get Anna back, but when I saw her again the reality of her needs and her disability became clear. No matter how much I'd wished and hoped that her situation was different than it was, I knew that day that the reality was I was not ready to care for her in the way she needed, and that her needs were greater than I'd been willing to admit to myself. That was also the day I met her future adoptive mom in person. It was then that I realized that Rebekah was meant to be Anna's mom. I saw that she loved my daughter and that my daughter loved her, and I knew that was how it was supposed to be. I was too ashamed to admit it to anyone but myself at that point, but that was the day I knew. I did not walk in with the intention of making that kind of decision, but that was the day I can look back on and see that my choice was made.

When I saw Rebekah loving my daughter, it was wonderful. I felt relieved because it was what Anna deserved. Even though I couldn't be there for her, she was getting what she needed and everything she deserved. She had a mom; someone loved her. In spite of my shame for myself, I felt grateful seeing someone else loving her and knowing that my daughter loved her back.

I did not doubt my choice, though I was afraid we might lose touch and that I wouldn't be able to participate in seeing my daughter grow up. It was what I needed to do for her, but it was scary to let go and trust that we would remain in contact. You hear stories of mothers who let their children be adopted and then things change between them and the adoptive family—I was secretly worried that might happen. I also worried about how my family would react and what they would think. Ultimately, though, it didn't matter because I knew it was her life that would be impacted. I saw hope for Anna. For myself, I felt gratitude, comfort, and relief at what I could now give her. There was no comfort for myself in the fact that I gave her up, but I had to do right by her. I still face the shame that it had to be that way.

I know God gave me the peace to make the decision I made, and I see His hand in it. If not for that, I know I never would've made that decision because of the treatment I would receive later and how people would view me and my choice. But I would've given her a meager life at best, and I know she has more now than I could've provided for her.

Because of God, my heart is open to the relationships I have with Anna's adoptive parents and my other kids' former foster parents. I should have become a closed, hateful, nonloving, untrusting person, but I know God allowed me to have this peace about who they are and that they love my kids.

The only thing I would change about my story, truthfully, is that I never would have used drugs and that Anna wouldn't have been born in the circumstance she was. I wouldn't change that I allowed her to be adopted or that I chose Rebekah and Aaron to be her parents. I knew there was a strong likelihood that we could have a friendship, and I love Rebekah for having the strength and courage to ask me if they could adopt Anna.

The more I talk with Rebekah, the more she hits notes that allow me to see God in my life. I remember meeting her and seeing how open, loving, and caring she was and having this feeling of peace. Later she related to me that Aaron was changed as a result of adopting Anna. I can see that God's hand was on this whole situation and that this was His plan from the beginning. It's like God letting me know He was there; He was the reason for the peace I felt, even in the midst of my pain. I feel lost and rarely have peace with decisions I make, but when I do have that peace, I know it was from God. I know God is there, I believe in Him, I feel Him, but I think He is just waiting for me to take the steps I need to take to come to Him.

I remember the day when Anna was about eight months old that I picked up the phone to call my friend Whitney, Anna's physical therapist, about adoption. I dialed her number, made a little bit of small talk, breathed in deeply, heart pounding (I knew Whitney would tell me what she really thought), and asked, "So, what would you say if I told you I think maybe we are supposed to consider adopting Anna?"

She did not hesitate. "I'd say you're crazy," she replied.

We discussed all of the uncertainties, the fact that Anna might require full-time nursing care even into adulthood, the fact that her mental abilities might not be typical, what our lives would look like, what Anna's life would look like. And then she told me that if I really felt like the prompting was from the Lord, I shouldn't ignore it.

I should have been terrified. I probably should just have had a good chuckle and prayed that someone a lot more qualified would come along and decide to make Anna part of their family. Maybe I should even have thought of all the ways that our ministry (volunteering, involvement in church programs, missions, etc.) would be limited if we walked down this path. Perhaps I should even have worried that this whole thing would open up the floodgates and lead us into a life very far from ordinary.

Looking back, I still cannot figure out how I got from there to here. I don't completely understand why I listened to the prompting and ignored every reason that we were nuts to even consider such a proposition. It still borders on incomprehensible that God would have chosen to use me to be a part of this story. That He would take this beautiful, broken little girl and make me her mama. And that He would make an even more beautiful story out of the brokenness of a whole situation that would later scream of His glory to anyone who would listen.

And the floodgates have opened. About a year after we adopted Anna, we learned of another little girl in foster care who needed a family. My friend sent me a photo with the caption "Adopt me," and I immediately wanted to know more. I knew her foster mom. We met Abigail and proceeded to jump over every hurdle and challenge the system could throw at us. We were told that we couldn't receive special treatment just because we'd met her. I didn't want special treatment; I just wanted them to consider us as a possible family for her. I made phone calls; I tried to talk to anyone who could help us walk through an out-of-state adoption through foster care. On the day of her MATCH meeting, they immediately dismissed our family as a possibility. Then a gentleman I'd spoken to over the phone who was providentially assigned to her case begged them to revisit our family as a viable option. Her foster mom pleaded our case because she knew we'd keep her in Abigail's life. They wanted to move along to other families in the state that would make for a far less complicated placement. God had other plans. We were matched.

It was not over, though. Months later, I went to Florida (we'd since relocated to another state) and lived there for two months with Anna in order to work on a transition plan for Abigail to allow her to prepare for being part of our family. At the eleventh hour, we were told she would not be coming with us. I made more phone calls, I pleaded, and we were granted a provision to leave the state but told we might need to return within a month and then again every month until the paperwork was completed.

The day before we were to be required to return to the state, we got a phone call that they'd completed the necessary documents and that she could remain with us in our home state. A couple months later, our adoption was finalized. And the adventure of the first year with a two-year-old who'd just lost the only mother and family she'd known began. I read and learned and prayed and cried through that year, and I worked and worked to help my baby girl through her grief and through the process of learning to attach to us.

About a year after her adoption was finalized, we prayed for a baby. Through a bizarre set of circumstances, we got a phone call about a baby boy needing a family. We met and picked him up the next day. He was our son for two beautiful weeks, and then his mother asked us to give him back. We had been told, by a friend of hers, that she was not interested in her children and did not want to parent them. Samuel did not return to his mother but remained with the friend. Through a long and very difficult three months, we waited. One day, I knew it was time to act. I'd reached out to his mother after learning that she, in reality, loved her children very much, and she asked me to come to court with her. The rest of the story could fill several chapters of this book, but suffice it to say that it is a miracle the court determined that he would return to us. We have spent the last year and a half getting to know and love his mom. The craziest part of his story is that we knew, walking into it, that it was a possibility for everything to happen that did happen. I knew I might meet and fall in love with a baby I considered mine, only to have to give him up. We knew, and we did it anyway. It's messy and scary and a little bit strange. And we'd do it again.

I started to love a precious little girl, and before I knew it, I loved her mother, her sister, a brother, and his birth mother as well. We put one foot in front of the other, walked through the doors that didn't close, and were led through some of the most anguishing experiences and deepest grief imaginable, only to find that God had made this beautiful mess into a picture that others would love to see, and because of it, that they would want to know more about Him.

Our story is big. Our children's stories are big. They continue to be written. They are messy and strange and scary. People often look at us in shock and concern when we tell them parts of it. We speak of a God who passionately pursues us. He got messy for us. He picked us up out of our desperate situations with nothing at all to offer Him, and He adopted us. Just like we are.

Chapter 10

Response to Scripture's Teachings on Adoption

What should our response be to God's act of redeeming us from darkness and bringing us into His family? The scriptural call is clear.[131] First, we should read and search Scripture to understand how it instructs our lives. Everything we do and every thought we have should have its origins in a proper understanding of Scripture. Responding with our minds first will prepare us to respond with our hearts. Sermons can be given on the doctrine of adoption to inform congregations about their relationship to one another, and this understanding can help build the Christian community. Small groups can study our adoption in Christ and build each other up in the faith. The local church can focus on creating an orphan-friendly culture that meets the needs of its members and the fatherless in its locality. Pastors and small group leaders can lead the way through teaching about the social need to care for orphans in a way that is driven by the theological command to do so. The recent book *Orphanology*, by Tony Merida and Rick Morton, contains many ideas and resources that address the practical aspects of implementing orphan care.

Next, we can look inward and see the need that exists within our local churches in the persons of single mothers. We can reach out to help the fatherless created through divorce and unwed mothers within the local church. Parachurch organizations can be formed that provide nurture and support to single mothers and children in the foster care system. Churches can start local efforts to care for children in the foster system. Small groups can adopt a single mother or widow in the church and provide help and support when needed. These are but a few ideas for starting points. This should all be driven by an understanding of what God has done for us and not done solely as "good works."

---

131. Some Bible references include Exodus 22:22; Deuteronomy 27:19; Lamentations 5:3; Isaiah 1:23, 9:17, 10:2; Jeremiah 5:28; Ezekiel 22:7; Zechariah 7:10; Matthew 3:5; Job 6:27, 22:9, 24:3, 29:12, 31:17–18, 31:21; Deuteronomy 16:11,14; 24:17, 19–21; 26:12–13; 10:18; Jeremiah 7:6, 22:3, 49:11; Proverbs 23:10; Hosea 14:3; John 14:18; James 1:17; Romans 8:15, 23; 9:4; Galatians 4:5; Ephesians 1:5.

In our society, the mothers who either choose to give up their children or are forced to do so are often forgotten. Usually, these women are effectively fatherless. They can be unwed teens, single moms in abusive situations or with legal problems, strung up on drugs or homeless—to list just a few common circumstances. All these situations create fatherless women giving birth to fatherless children. Families who will love their children and at the same time reach out to them and show them the gospel through acts of selfless love can transform these young women's lives and preach the gospel to them in a way no pastor or sermon can.

Next, we should recognize that adoption is a calling and not something every Christian should do, just as not every Christian is called to be a pastor. However, every Christian is called to help with the care of the orphan and fatherless, just as all believers are instructed to share the gospel. This can include a myriad of things: mission trips with your church, going to overseas orphanages and rocking babies who have never been held, being involved with foster care, or financially supporting those who are called to adopt but can't afford the expense to do so.

Many church leaders do not know what local resources exist for orphan care and are unable to provide them to their members. They should educate themselves. When pastors do premarital counseling, they can and should include issues such as infertility and adoption in the topics discussed. Some statistics say that up to one in five couples will deal with infertility. Pastors should prepare newlyweds for this reality and give them a way in which God can be glorified in their difficulty and the world can see the church in action.

Below is a brief listing of possible resources as a starting point for involvement in orphan care.

- Sponsor an orphan with Children's Hope Chest.
- Find a widow or single mother and help with basic needs (for example, mowing the yard).
- Have your small group adopt a single mother or widow to help when needed.
- Become a foster parent.
- Get involved with organizations that help find families and provide funds or accept donations for international children with special needs, such as the Shepherd's Crook, Bethany Christian Services, or Brittany's Hope Foundation.

- Read books for your education and to discover other ways to help: *Fields of the Fatherless, Reclaiming Adoption, Orphanology: Awakening to Gospel-Centered Adoption and Orphan Care.*

The church is in a struggle with the world for the souls of the fatherless. The number of orphans worldwide is increasing exponentially. The doctrine of adoption has lain dormant for centuries, and we have forgotten our adoption through Christ into the family of God. This has affected our ability to see our calling in God to be the defenders of the fatherless here on earth.

The struggle will not be small. The expense of adoption alone discourages many from attempting it. Our cultural fixation on genetic heritage has caused us to lose sight of the reality that strong families can be made through adoption and need not be made through technology. Current technological trends are encouraging scientific procedures for fertility issues and indirectly discouraging adoption. Government intervention through foster care has become the mainstay of orphan care in our country. European laws are in the making that will prevent adoption by Christian couples due to the concern that those couples will affect the self-identify of the adoptee through religious indoctrination. UNICEF's official policy on adoption discourages adoption and considers it only as a last resort.[132] A recent result of their policy has been the closing of Guatemala (and many other countries) to outside adoption.[133] Here in the US, homosexual lobby groups are actively working to legalize adoption for same-sex couples. Is the church going to continue to relegate this ministry to society at large, or are we going to reclaim adoption?

"Pure and undefiled religion in the sight of our God and Father is this: to visit orphans and widows in their distress and to keep oneself unstained by the world." —James 1:27

"Learn to do good; seek justice, reprove the ruthless, defend the orphan, plead for the widow." —Isaiah 1:17

---

132. UNICEF, "UNICEF's Position on Inter-country Adoption."
133. Guatemala's closing to foreign adoption is a complex issue, but in the end it closed to external adoption after pressure from UNICEF.

Conclusion

Despite the importance of the doctrine of adoption in the Bible, it has been sorely neglected in the development of both biblical and systematic theology. Over time, this lack has led to a general neglect in adoption's relation to practical theology as well, with a resultant lack of its application to the life of the church. The result is that the church at large has left the practice of orphan care largely neglected. Yet, this doctrine can be seen throughout Scriptures. The first hint or seeds of it are seen in Genesis, it becomes clearer as God redeems Israel out of Egypt, the legal mandates for orphan care thereafter are found in the Law and the Prophets, and finally, its full understanding is revealed in the New Testament.

Paul's understanding of adoption is best understood in the context of the kingdom of God as made up of God's sons and daughters. The typology of Israel as God's son, which Paul applied to the church, further shows his understanding that this thread goes from the Old Testament to the New. As one reads from Genesis to Malachi, there is a change in emphasis from the nation of Israel to the individual members in the nation and their relationship with God.[134] Paul's stress on adoption is closely related to his teachings on the first and second Adams. Both Adams affected our relationship to the Father. The first (Adam) forfeited the status that he originally possessed, and the second (Jesus), through His work on the cross, restored this relationship (Romans 5:12; 1 Corinthians 15:23, 45; Romans 1:3; Galatians 2:20; Ephesians 4:13).

Paul viewed our adoptive status as a present part of our salvation, sealed with the Holy Spirit. Through the seal of the Spirit, the future completion of our adoption becomes guaranteed. The eschatological tension heightens our sense of longing for our future home while providing us confidence in this present world of our hope and salvation found only in Christ. We learn from Paul that our adoption in Christ was predestined as part of God's eternal will. The process of adoption includes the whole Trinity. The Father wills, the Son redeems, and the Spirit seals. From Paul's teachings, we gain insight from which we can see how the doctrine of adoption is inclusive of the whole of Scripture.

---

134. Theron, "'Adoption' in the Pauline corpus," 8–10.

From this vantage point, we can appreciate more fully how the apostle John viewed our salvation. He viewed our experience relationally. His emphasis on regeneration focused on our joining Jesus in His relationship with the Father. As we share in this with Jesus, we become sons of the Most High God. John did not identify adoption as the mode of family inclusion, but it is clear that the relationship formed is that of sons. In his epistles we see love as the bond of the brotherhood of believers, and we learn that without this love of the brethren, no one can have fellowship with the Father. John even goes so far as to state that our love for one another will be a sign to the world that the Father has sent the Son. In Revelation, we learn that God names those He has called, an act similar to what happens to orphans adopted by Roman patrons.

God has been in the process of naming those He calls out from the beginning. He changed Abraham's name right before the birth of Isaac to signify his new destiny. God similarly changed Jacob's name to Israel after He wrestled with him. Israel later was identified with the nation that God claimed as His son. God delivered the Israelites, brought them to Mount Sinai, gave them the Law, and then proceeded to disciple the nation as His son throughout the remainder of the Old Testament. Within the Law and the Prophets are embedded commands to protect the orphan and widow. God identifies Himself as the Father to the fatherless and commands His nation to do as He has done—protect and defend the fatherless. God is expressing the theological reality of His identity as Father of the fatherless through practical laws to protect them.

Jesus also picks up this theme in the gospels. It is epitomized in the judgment of Matthew 25. The judgment at Christ's second return is intimately linked to care for the least of these—Jesus equates caring for them with caring for Him. The Son of Man will bring the nations before Himself and judge them based on their care for the least of these, those whom He equates as His brothers.

As we look at all of these things, the power and importance of the doctrine of adoption becomes clear. It brings together disparate people—Jews and Gentiles. Adoption includes an eternal inheritance that looks toward the future. Adoption is sealed by the Holy Spirit. It starts with Israel and Israel's king and finds its fulfillment in Christ and His new brethren. It spans the whole of the Scriptures and touches on a remarkable range of biblical themes. Adoption transcends ethical and biological boundaries and shows God's working from the foundation of the world to include us in His family. Through adoption, we learn that our identity does not rest with us but with God who makes us His own, calls us by name, and in the end will give us a name that only He knows. It points to the present reality of God's grace and the future promise of participation in His glory. Adoption sheds light on our election; though we may wander and suffer correction, our Father will pour out His very self to ensure that we will never be let go.

The unresolved question is this: how will we respond? Does our theology change the very core of our beings, or does it only inform our minds? Does our thinking the thoughts of God and knowing His eternal will change our minds and wills? Should we copy in earthly things what our Father has done in heavenly things? Should we mirror in this world what God has started for us in this one and will finish in the world to come? Preaching the gospel through living it out is a powerful and undeniable witness. People can argue about theology, creationism, and other issues, but they can't argue about your life. Preaching the gospel at all times and using words when necessary, as Francis of Assisi is purported to have said, has deep significance. Our lives are to be a living sacrifice, holy and acceptable to Him, not just our words.

The early church lived out the gospel in a way that changed Roman society, and doing so can change ours today. Jesus promised us that He will not leave us as orphans—He will come to us (John 14:18). What better example is there in this world of what God has done for us than care for the orphan? And if there is none, how do we respond?

Bibliography

Anders, Max. *Galatians-Colossians.* Vol. 8. Holman New Testament Commentary. Nashville: Broadman & Holman Publishers, 1999.

Bartlett, David L. "Adoption in the Bible." *The Child in the Bible,* eds. Marcia J Bunge, Terence E. Fretheim, and Beverly Roberts Gaventa. Grand Rapids, MI: Eerdmans, 2008.

Benson, Peter, Anu Sharma, and Eugene Roehlkepartain. *Growing up Adopted: A Portrait of Adolescents and Their Families.* Minneapolis, MN: The Search Institute, 1984.

Boa, K. & W. Kruidenier. Romans. Vol. 6. Holman New Testament Commentary. Nashville: Broadman & Holman Publishers, 2000.

Braeutigam, Michael. "Adopted by the Triune God, The Doctrine of Adoption from a Trinitarian Perspective." *Scottish Bulletin of Evangelical Theology.* August 16, 2009.

Burke, Trevor J. "Pauline Adoption: a Sociological Approach," *Evangelical Quarterly 73,* no 2. (Apr 2001): 119–134.

Calvin, John. *Epistle of Paul the Apostle to the Romans.* Trans. by John Owen. Edinburgh: Calvin Translation Society, 1849.
—*Institutes of the Christian Religion.* Edited by John T. McNeil. Trans. by Ford Lewis Battles. Vols. 1 & 2. Philadelphia: The Westminster Press, 1960.
—*The Gospel According to St. John 1–10.* Trans. T.H.L. Parker. Edinburgh: Oliver and Boyd, 1959.

Candlish, Rob. S. *The Fatherhood of God. Being the First Course of the Cunningham Lectures.* Edinburgh: Adam and Charles Black, 1867.

Cruver, Dan, John Piper, Scotty Smith, Richard Phillips, and Jason Kovacs. *Reclaiming Adoption: Missional Living Through the Rediscovery of Abba Father.* Adelphi, MD: Cruciform Press, 2011.

Davis, Tom. *Fields of the Fatherless.* Colorado Springs: David C. Cook Publishers, 2008.

Duffield, G. P. & N.M. Van Cleave. *Foundations of Pentecostal Theology*. Los Angles: L.I.F.E. Bible College, 1983.

Dunn, James. "Spirit Speech: Reflections on Romans 8:12–27." *Romans and the People of God*, eds. Sven Soderlund and N. T. Wright. Grand Rapids, MI: Eerdmans, 1999.

Freeman, James M. and Harold J. Chadwick. *Manners & Customs of the Bible*. Rev. ed. North Brunswick, NJ: Bridge-Logos Publishers, 1998.

Ferguson, Sinclair. *Children of the Living God*. Edingburgh, UK: The Banner of Truth Trust, 1989.

Frame, John M. *The Doctrine of the Knowledge of God*. Phillipsburg, New Jersey: Presbyterian and Reformed Publishing Company, 1987.

Guthrie, Donald. *New Testament Introduction*. 4th ed. Downers Grove, IL: InterVarsity Press, 1990.

Girardeau, John L. *Discussions of Theological Questions*. Harrisonburg, VA: Sprinkle Publications, 1986.

Henry, Matthew. *Matthew Henry's Commentary on the Whole Bible in One Volume*. Grand Rapids, MI: Zondervan Publishing House, 1960.

Hodge, Charles. *Systematic Theology*. Vols. 2 & 3. Oak Harbor, WA: Logos Research Systems, 1997.

Johnson, Elizabeth Ann. "Waiting for Adoption: Reflections on Romans 8:12–25." *Word and World* 22, no 3. (2002): 308–312.

Keller, Timothy. *The Prodigal God: Recovering the Heart of the Christian Faith*. New York: Dutton Publishing, 2008.

Kelly, Douglas F. "Adoption: An Underdeveloped Heritage of the Westminster Standards," *Reformed Theological Review* 52, no. 3. (1993): 110–120.

Kelly, Douglas, Hugh McClure, and Philip Rollinson. *The Westminster Confession of Faith: An Authentic Modern Version*. Signal Mountain, TN: Summertown Texts, 1992.

Kirby, Gilbert W. "God's adoption procedure," *Christianity Today* 17, no. 19. (1973): 14–15.

Koester, Helmut. *History, Culture and Religion of the Hellenistic Age.* Berlin: Walter de Gruyter, 1995.

Lidgett, J.S. *The Fatherhood of God in Christian Truth and Life.* Edinburgh: T&T Clark, 1902.

Lloyd-Jones, David Martyn. *God the Holy Spirit.* Wheaton, IL.: Crossway Books, 1997.
—*God the Father, God the Son.* Wheaton, IL.: Crossway Books, 1996.

Lyall, Francis. "Roman Law in the Writing of Paul—Adoption," *Journal of Biblical Literature* 88, no. 4. (1969): 458–466.

Moore, Russell D. *Adopted for Life: The Priority of Adoption for Christian Families.* Wheaton, IL: Crossway Books, 2009.
—"Abba Changes Everything: Why every Christian is called to rescue Orphans," *Christianity Today* 54, no. 7. (2010): 18–42.

Mounce, Robert H. *Romans.* The New American Commentary. 31 vols. Electronic ed. Logos Library System. Nashville: Broadman & Holman Publishers, 2001.

Myers, Allen C. *The Eerdmans Bible Dictionary.* Grand Rapids, MI: Eerdmans, 1987.

Nydam, Ronald J. "Adoption and the Image of God," *The Journal of Pastoral Care* 46, no. 3. (1992): 247–260.

Packer, J. I. *Concise Theology : A Guide to Historic Christian Beliefs.* Wheaton, IL: Tyndale House, 1995.
—*Knowing God.* Downers Grove, IL: InterVarsity Press, 1993.

Post, Stephen G. "Adoption Theologically Considered," *Journal of Religious Ethics* 24, no. 1. (1997): 149–168.

Rossell, William H. "New Testament Adoption—Graeco-Roman or Semitic?", *Journal of Biblical Literature* 71, no. 4. (1952): 233–235.

Ryrie, Charles Caldwell. *A Survey of Bible Doctrine*. Chicago: Moody Press, 1995.

Schmidt, Alvin J. *How Christianity Changed the World*. Grand Rapids, MI: Zondervan Publishing, 2004.

Shedd, William Greenough Thayer and Alan W. Gomes. *Dogmatic Theology*. 3rd ed. Phillipsburg, NJ: P & R Pub, 2003.

Strong, Augustus Hopkins. *Systematic Theology*. Vol. 2. Bellingham, WA: Logos Research Systems, 2004.

Theron, Daniel J. "'Adoption' in the Pauline corpus," *Evangelical Quarterly* 28, no. 1. (1956): 6–14.

Tillich, Paul. *The Courage to Be*. New Haven, CT: Yale University Press, 1952.

Trumper, Tim. "The Metaphorical Import of Adoption : A Plea for Realisation," *Scottish Bulletin of Evangelical Theology* (14 Aug 1996): 129–145.
—"A Fresh Exposition of Adoption. I: An Outline," *Scottish Bulletin of Evangelical Theology* 23, no 1 (2005): 60–80.
—"The Theological History of Adoption. I: An Account," *Scottish Bulletin on Evangelical Theology* 20, no. 1 (2002): 4–28.
— "The Theological History of Adoption, II: A Rationale," *Scottish Bulletin on Evangelical Theology* 20, no.2. (2002): 177–202.

UNICEF. *The State of the World's Children 2006: Excluded and Invisible*. PDF report. http://www.unicef.org/sowc06/pdfs/sowc06_fullreport. pdf. 2006.
—"UNICEF's Position on Inter-country Adoption," http://www.unicef. org/media/media_41918.html. 2010.
—"Who Are the Invisible?" http://www.unicef.org/sowc06/press/who. php. 2006.

Vellanickal, M. "The Divine Sonship of Christians in the Johannine Writing," *Analecta Biblica* 72. Rome: Biblical Institute, 1977.

Webb, Robert Alexander. *The Reformed Doctrine of Adoption.* Grand Rapids, MI: WM.B. Eerdmans Publishing, 1947.

Westhead, Nigel. "Adoption in the Thought of John Calvin," *Scottish Bulletin of Evangelical Theology.* (13 Aug 1995): 102–115.

Wiersbe, W. W. *The Bible Exposition Commentary.* Wheaton, IL: Victor Books, 1996.

Yeats, John M. "The Biblical Model of Adoption," *Southwestern Journal of Theology* 49, no. 1 (2006): 65–79.

Visit us on Facebook:
Adopted: God's "Plan A"
www.facebook.com/AdoptedGodsPlanA